GUITAR WORLD PRESENTS

PINK FLOYD

From the pages of
GUITAR WORLD
magazine

Compiled by
Alan di Perna

Edited by
Jeff Kitts and Brad Tolinski

HAL•LEONARD®

Published in cooperation with Harris Publications, Inc., and *Guitar World* magazine
Guitar World is a registered trademark of Harris Publications, Inc.

Cover photos: Top — Govert De Roos/London Features
     Bottom left — Ross Marino/London Features
     Bottom right — Michael Putland/London Features

Published by Hal Leonard Corporation
7777 West Bluemound Road
P.O. Box 13819
Milwaukee, WI 53213, USA

Trade Book Division Editorial Offices:
151 West 46th Street, 8th Floor
New York, NY 10036

Visit Hal Leonard online at **www.halleonard.com**

Library of Congress Cataloging-in-Publication Data

Guitar world presents Pink Floyd / compiled by Alan di Perna ;
edited by Jeff Kitts and Brad Tolinski.– 1st ed.
  p. cm.
ISBN 0-634-03286-0
1. Pink Floyd (Musical quartet) 2. Rock musicians–England–Biography.
3. Rock music–History and criticism.
I. Title: Pink FLoyd. II. Di Perna, Alan, 1953- III. Kitts, Jeff. IV.
Tolinski, Brad. V. Guitar world.
 ML421.P6 G85 2002
 782.42166'092'2--dc21
                   2002007433

Printed in the United States of America
First edition

10 9 8 7 6 5 4 3 2 1

Table of Contents

Pink Floyd, the original lineup, in 1967. *Left to right*: Roger Waters, Syd Barrett, Nick Mason, Richard Wright.

Guitar World, December 2001

Mysterious Ways

Mind-bending psychedelia. Breathtaking live shows. Million-selling albums. This is the inside story of Pink Floyd, rock's most cosmic entity.

By Alan di Perna

THE SUN NEVER SETS ON PINK FLOYD

Pink Floyd are, in many ways, the most unlikely members of the classic rock pantheon. They were never heavy like Led Zeppelin or rowdy like the Who, or sexual like Hendrix or even as controversial as the Beatles during their "bigger than Jesus" and LSD years. For most of Pink Floyd's lengthy tenure on the rock scene, the band's members have behaved like perfect English gentlemen. How many other rock stars can claim that? Even the Floyd's notoriously bitter feuds were completely non-violent. I once asked David Gilmour if any of the band's legendary squabbles ever ended in a punch-up. He seemed quietly horrified at the suggestion.

Despite Pink Floyd's unwillingness to act up like regular rock stars, the band's music, lyrics and imagery have ingrained themselves deeply in the hearts, minds and souls of classic rock fans. Every metal palooka who has ever played yearning pentatonics over a non-blues chord progression invariably tells the guitar press he was "going for a David Gilmour thing." Not a Carlos Santana thing, mind you. Not a Mick Ronson thing, or a Ritchie Blackmore, Alvin Lee or Bill Nelson thing. Of all the Seventies guitar greats, the affable, understated Mr. Gilmour has come to represent the broad sweep of Seventies, pre-Van Halen guitar stylistics for the general rock public of the early 21st century.

Beyond that, Pink Floyd albums like *Dark Side of the Moon* and *The Wall* have become a rite of passage for numerous generations. There's something in Roger Waters' bleak, aggrieved lyrics that encapsulates the uneasy transition from adolescence to early adulthood. And the Floyd's floaty, dreamy music has the power to evoke those inward journeys of imagination that sustain us all our lives.

The story of how Pink Floyd came to be unlikely titans of classic rock is a tale of madness, mishaps and happy accidents—as compelling as any of the band's hugely successful albums.

CHAPTER ONE: THE SYD BARRETT YEARS (1965–68)

In the long history of Pink Floyd, one figure looms large. Syd Barrett recorded only one album and a handful of singles with the group, but he was Pink Floyd's original leader and guiding light. He has become a cult figure for rock aficionados. It was Barrett who named Pink Floyd, who wrote all the band's early hits and who provided them with a focal point. In all the years that followed Syd's descent into madness and his 1968 departure from Pink Floyd, the group would never again have quite such a charismatic, enigmatic front man. Barrett defined Pink Floyd's first incarnation. And his absence became the black hole around which Pink Floyd's latter-day identity coalesced.

Like Banquo's ghost, Syd was the unseen specter standing behind Roger Waters as he assumed leadership of Pink Floyd in the early Seventies. Barrett formed the subject matter for many of Waters' greatest triumphs with Floyd, including *Dark Side of the Moon* and *Wish You Were Here*. And even though *The Wall* is ostensibly Waters' great autobiographical opus, it's not hard to find echoes of Syd in the portrayal of a rock star's withdrawal into catatonic solipsism throughout his career. Waters has explored the idea of abnormal psychology—of what happens when a person strays beyond the boundary of what we think of as sanity. But it was Syd who actually crossed that line.

The picturesque British university town of Cambridge was the birthplace of Roger Waters (September 9, 1943), David Gilmour (March 4, 1947) and Roger Keith Barrett (January 6, 1946), who acquired the nickname Syd early in life. While many of the legendary English rock bands came from the working class, the members of

Pink Floyd all grew up comfortably middle class. The family of drummer Nick Mason (January 27, 1945) was actually quite affluent. From them the drummer acquired a lifelong passion for world-class racing cars—and something of a playboy dilettante reputation. Meanwhile, Roger Waters' upper-middle-class aloofness would earn him a reputation as rock's biggest snob.

Two years older than Syd Barrett, Waters would drop by the Barrett household in Cambridge and listen to Syd's teenage band, the Mottoes. One thing Barrett and Waters had in common was that they both lost their fathers. Eric Fletcher Waters, an RAF airman, was killed in combat over Italy during WWII, just months after the birth of his son Roger. Growing up in the absence of a father he never knew has had a profound effect on Roger Waters' life and work. It's a topic he dealt with directly in *The Wall*. And much of his work is steeped in a deep-rooted contempt for the military mind-set in all its lethal stupidity.

Syd Barrett lost his father at the age of 14. The sudden death of Dr. Max Barrett, an eminent police pathologist, was the first in a series of traumatic events that would ultimately trigger what many feel was a genetic proclivity toward insanity in his son Syd. Another psychologically damaging episode came in 1966, when Syd was in his early twenties. At that time—about a year before the Beatles discovered Maharishi Mahesh Yogi—Barrett and a group of his friends became immersed in an Indian spiritual path called Sant Mat. But Syd was devastated on being rejected for initiation by the group's leader, Maharaji Charan Singh Ji. According to those close to him, he took it as a sign of some profound, cosmic unworthiness on his part.

By that point, however, Barrett was at art school in London, and he had already joined forces with a fledging rock band formed by Waters, Nick Mason and keyboardist Rick Wright (b. July 28, 1945), all three of whom were studying architecture in Britain's capital. Originally named Sigma 6, they tried calling themselves the T-Set, the Megadeaths, the Architectural Abdabs, and the Screaming Abdabs, before Barrett came up with the Pink Floyd Sound, grafting the name of two obscure American blues musicians, Pink Anderson and Floyd Council.

The Pink Floyd Sound played their first gig under that name in 1965, at London's Countdown Club. Initially, the repertoire consisted of the standard rock and r&b covers that bands played back then. But from the start, Barrett, Waters, Wright and Mason would expand the middle of songs with protracted and abstract instrumental improvisations which quickly reached far beyond blues-based riffing. These improvised soundscapes often included random elements such as radio broadcasts and the sound of ball bearings being rolled down guitar strings to create arresting harmonic overtones. Many of these techniques had been pioneered by an earlier experimental art group, AAM, who had been managed by Peter Jenner, the man who became manager of the Pink Floyd Sound.

As early as 1966, Pink Floyd live performances incorporated the use of film, which was projected onto a backdrop at the rear of the stage and onto the musicians themselves, adding a visual element that had never before been seen at live rock and roll shows. A flair for elaborate visual effects in live performance would become a constant factor in Pink Floyd's shifting identity over the years. They were the first rock group to employ their own full-time lighting director (Joe Gannon), whose craft was closely coordinated with the group's music.

"If we have to have some kind of definition, you can say we are lights and sounds," Syd Barrett told journalists at the time. "The two mediums complement each other, and we definitely don't use them together as a gimmick. Our aim is simply to make the audience dig the effect."

The Pink Floyd's emergence on the London scene coincided with the arrival of psychedelia from San Francisco, far away on America's West Coast. Barrett, Waters, Wright and Mason were at the vanguard of an incredible wave of British psychedelic bands, a kaleidoscopic burst of one-hit wonders and enduring talents chronicled on Rhino Records' *Nuggets II* box set. Swinging London put its own spin on psychedelia. Filmmakers, poets, people from the avant-garde theater and visual arts joined forces with rock musicians to make the London scene a colorful—and arguably more cosmopolitan—counterpart to what the American hippies were up to over in the City by the Bay.

The Pink Floyd (having dropped the Sound from their name) became the pied pipers of British psychedelia. Members of the Beatles, filmmaker Michelangelo Antonioni and other international celebs were spotted at their gigs. They became the de facto house band at the UFO club, London's fave freakout spot, which got started

The Madcap Laughs: Syd Barrett in 1967.

Ray Stevenson/Retna

in December of '66. There they alternated with acts like the Soft Machine, the Crazy World of Arthur Brown, Procol Harum and Tomorrow (the latter featuring guitarist Steve Howe, later of Yes.) The Pink Floyd were also a favored attraction at marathon happenings like the 14 Hour Technicolor Dream, held on April 29, 1967. These were, in essence, the first raves.

"We've been hired by so many of these freakout merchants," said Waters at the time, with characteristic detachment. "I sometimes think that it's only because we have lots of equipment and lighting and it saves the promoters from having to hire lighting for the group."

With such a hot local buzz on them, it wasn't long before the Pink Floyd were signed to a record deal, with EMI in England. Their debut single was "Arnold Layne," recorded in January 1967 and released in March of that year. With "Arnold" and its B side, "Candy and a Currant Bun," Syd Barrett came to the fore as the group's songwriter. Whimsical and melodic, "Arnold Layne" helped set the pattern of a specifically British brand of psychedelic pop. The title character being a kleptomaniac transvestite—Arnold likes to steal ladies' clothes from washing lines—the single stirred up some controversy in staid Britain as well.

"I was at Cambridge when I started to write the song," Barrett recalled. "I thought Arnold Layne was a nice name and it fitted very well into the music I had already composed. Then I thought, Arnold must have a hobby, and it went on from there. Arnold just happens to dig dressing up in women's clothing. A lot of people do, so let's face up to reality."

"Arnold Layne" was followed into the British charts by "See Emily Play" four months later. One of the most memorable discs of the psychedelic era, "Emily" reflects the childlike quality of Syd's imagination. It also spotlights his unique way with slide guitar. Light years removed from the standard blues lexicon, Syd's slide work had the ascendant character of a spaceship taking off. The "space rock" tag was one of many legacies from the Barrett era that would stay with Pink Floyd throughout their career. Syd's novel approach to slide was later taken up by David Gilmour. "See Emily Play" is a prime example of Barrett's ability to craft innovative, experimental songs that also happened to fulfill every requirement of the three-minute pop hit single. Sadly, this is one musical capability that left Pink Floyd when Syd did.

"Emily" was the lead track from the Pink Floyd's debut album, *Piper at the Gates of Dawn*. The title was taken from one of Syd's favorite children's novels, *The Wind in the Willows*. The album was recorded during the first half of 1967 at Abbey Road Studios. It was produced by Norman Smith, who had worked with the Beatles as an engineer under George Martin, and who didn't hesitate to plunge the Pink Floyd headlong into the kind of studio experimentation that worked so well for Martin and the Beatles. It proved to be just as suited to the Pink Floyd—perhaps even more so, given the group's firm basis in free-form improvisation.

The album boasts two extended instrumentals, "Pow R. Toc H." and the longtime live Floyd staple "Interstellar Overdrive." Many of the vocal numbers also include epic instrumental jams that showcase the freewheeling and precariously graceful interplay of Wright's Middle Eastern cadences on Farfisa combo organ, Waters' staccato bass lines, Mason's tribal thudding and Barrett's skewed, screeching, blipping and chirping guitar. Waters made one songwriting contribution to *Piper*, the characteristically dour "Take Up Thy Stethoscope and Walk." (Sample lyric: "Doctor Doctor, dark doom/Gruel ghoul greasy spoon.")

But the remaining 10 of the album's 11 songs were penned by Syd, whose compositions set a fanciful mood for the work as a whole. "Matilda Mother" has a fairytale quality. "Chapter 24" and "Scarecrow" exude tripped-out medievalism, while "Bike" is deliriously vaudevillian. In keeping with the pattern set by "Arnold Layne," these songs are peopled by an odd cast of characters: a gnome named Grimble Gromble, a mouse called Gerald, a mysterious cat named Lucifer Sam who is a familiar of the witch Jennifer Gentle. Barrett's lyrics revel in the company of imaginary friends.

Buoyed by the success of "Arnold Layne" and "See Emily Play," *Piper at the Gates of Dawn* made it to No. 6 in Britain. A truncated version of the album was released in the States, where it was more of an underground phenomenon. The original incarnation of Pink Floyd could have been bigger in the States had they done the kind of relentless touring and promotion that put other British groups over the top here. But that just wasn't in the cards. By the time *Piper* was released, in August 1967, Barrett's behavior had become even more erratic than what might be expected of your typical psychedelic pop star.

It is said that, of the original Floyd quartet, Waters and Mason were drinking men, while Wright and Barrett were into drugs. Few people embraced the hallucinogen LSD as enthusiastically as Barrett. He would trip for days and weeks on end, often unwittingly "dosed" by well-meaning friends. All this acid binging had a disastrous effect on Syd's already fragile psyche.

There were violent episodes with girlfriends, one of whom was kept locked in a room and held against her will for a week by the deranged Barrett. Syd's onstage performances grew increasingly incoherent. The other band members would have no idea what he was going to play, sing or do up there. There was a particularly muddled appearance at the International Love-In in London on July 29, 1967.

Barrett and Waters didn't only differ in their choice of intoxicants. They had opposing views on fame and commercial success as well. Waters wanted these things quite badly. Syd despised them, and would generally refuse to cooperate in any activity that stood the slightest chance of boosting record sales. For an appearance on *Top of the Pops*, Britain's leading music TV program, Syd turned up in full pop star regalia, only to change into scruffy clothing for the band's actual on-camera performance.

It didn't help matters that the band refused to play their hit singles, "Arnold Layne" or "See Emily Play," at live performances. Out in the provinces, punters who had turned out specifically to hear these tunes would often become violent when they were instead offered extended space jams and an incoherent front man. The Jimi Hendrix Experience toured with the Pink Floyd on one of these British junkets. Hendrix coined the epithet "Laughing Syd Barrett," in joking reference to Syd's catatonic state.

The situation worsened during the Pink Floyd's one tour of America with Syd in late 1967. He refused to lip-synch on *American Bandstand*, standing there blankly as the track played. And on Pat Boone's show, a catatonic stare was Barrett's only reply to interview questions posed by the show's feckless host.

By the beginning of 1968, Waters, Mason and Wright had reluctantly decided to dismiss Syd. "We tried to keep Syd going for as long as possible," Waters recently stated. "I really wanted Syd to become what Brian Wilson was in the Beach Boys—for him to stay in the band and keep writing songs, but not to perform with the band. But it wasn't to be. He kind of had other ideas, and so did our manager at the time. But you know, the songwriter is the goose that lays the golden egg. And everybody recognizes that."

Syd went on to release two solo albums, *Barrett* and *The Madcap Laughs*, both of which are well worth investigating. (A collection of Syd outtakes, titled *Opel*, was released in 1988.) *Madcap* was produced by Waters and the man who was to become Syd's replacement in Pink Floyd, Dave Gilmour. *Barrett* was produced by Gilmour and Wright. Working with the erratic Syd was, by all accounts, a very difficult procedure. In one telling studio incident, Barrett—thinking he was being presented with a bill—bit the hand of a person who passed him a lyric sheet.

Sad anecdotes like these have done nothing to diminish the high esteem in which Syd Barrett is held by just about anyone with a rudimentary understanding of rock history. He was a huge influence on Marc Bolan, David Bowie and Robyn Hitchcock, among other key rock figures.

"When Syd Barrett left, there was no Pink Floyd for me anymore," Bowie has said.

Syd's early decline lends added poignancy to *Piper at the Gates of Dawn*. It is the one complete and whole work we have from a mind teetering precariously between genius and insanity. A true manifesto of the psychedelic era.

CHAPTER TWO:
THE REINVENTION OF PINK FLOYD (1968–71)

Right around the time of Syd Barrett's departure, the Pink Floyd dropped the definite article from their name, becoming simply Pink Floyd.

It was the end of an era, but the start of whole new phase in the band's career—one that would take them to far greater fame than they'd even known with Barrett. The guitarist who would see them into this era was a close friend of Syd's from the Cambridge days. David Gilmour came from a similarly comfortable background as the other members of Pink Floyd. His father was a prominent geneticist and his mother a film editor. Before joining forces with Pink Floyd, Dave had been playing with Jokers Wild, a rock and r&b cover band. Nearly the same age as Syd and reasonably good looking, his initial role was to cover Syd's guitar and vocal parts at live performances.

"We had to do something," Gilmour once told *Guitar World*. "It was either that or back to Bo Diddley covers."

Throughout the difficult process of Syd's mental collapse, the band had been struggling to record a follow-up to *Piper at the Gates of Dawn*. Gilmour joined this work in progress. Norman Smith was once again at the production helm. Released on June 29th, 1968, *Saucerful of Secrets* retains much the same psychedelic flavor as *Piper*. The disc contains two longer, improvisational pieces that would become standard components of Pink Floyd's live repertoire. "Set the Controls for the Heart of the Sun" was penned by Waters and revolves around a vaguely Arabic bass ostinato. Waters is generally crediting with pulling Pink Floyd together in the months after Syd's departure, his strong will to succeed establishing him in a de facto leadership role. *Saucerful of Secrets'* group-written title track—a lengthy and dense excursion into the outer limits of abstract noise— also became a favorite at live performances.

In Barrett's absence, Waters and Wright shouldered most of the songwriting responsibilities on *Saucerful*. Wright contributed the pleasant psychedelic pop piece "Remember a Day." Waters weighed in with the anti-militaristic "Corporal Clegg," complete with a parodic kazoo marching band. Though deeply and personally felt, Waters' pacifist sentiments were also very much in tune with the peace-and-love mood of the late Sixties, an era of strong opposition to the Vietnam War. The period abounds in memorable anti-war tracks like Country Joe and Fish's "I-Feel-Like-I'm-Fixin'-to-Die Rag," the Doors' "The Unknown Soldier" and the Animals' "Sky Pilot."

The only Syd track to make it onto *Saucerful of Secrets* is the closing number, "Jugband Music." The composition meanders episodically, moving from brass band bits to weird interludes, as Syd delivers cryptic lyrics in his detached, fragile voice. "I wonder who can be writing this song?" he sings at one point. The track's positioning gives Syd the fittingly enigmatic last words on *Saucerful of Secrets*: "What exactly is a dream and what exactly is a joke?"

Concerned with more pragmatic musical questions, Syd's replacement settled into what would become a key role. Here at the start of his recording career with Pink Floyd, Dave Gilmour shows a highly sympathetic sense of how to orchestrate the band's compositions with guitar sounds and textures, from the wah-wah flutters that adorn Wright's "See-Saw" to the stabbing monotone guitar figure that drives the strident verses of the aforementioned "Corporal Clegg." Gilmour's soloing on *Saucerful* comes off as more blues-based and more coherent than Barrett's; technically more competent although not as wildly unpredictable.

Saucerful of Secrets met with an indifferent critical response at its time of release. It clearly suffers from the lack of Barrett's distinctive songwriting voice, a state of affairs that is made all the more apparent by the fact that *Saucerful* is in essentially the same psychedelic style as *Piper*. Pink Floyd's sophomore album is best viewed as a transitional work. They were on the way to a new image and musical identity.

That identity started to emerge at an outdoor concert in London's Hyde Park—the first rock show ever to be held there—on the day *Saucerful of Secrets* was released. This critically well-received concert is regarded as ushering in a new level of professionalism and spectacle in Pink Floyd's live shows. Their sound system was more advanced than what most rock bands were using. It featured the quadraphonic "azimuth coordinator," which allowed specific sounds to be panned anywhere in the listening area—behind the audience, over their heads, left, right or front and center. The effect was to encompass the audience, to draw them into a sensory experience enhanced by the show's lighting and visual effects. It seems obvious now, but this was an engaging new idea in rock presentation back then. Emphasis was drawn away from the personalities onstage—the rock stars—and placed instead on the larger-than-life experience created by music, sound and light. Which is what the group had been out to achieve all along in their live concerts. But now they had superior technology, and also a compelling reason to impart this sense of spectacle to their live performances. When they lost Syd, they lost their front man.

"We didn't have a Mick Jagger or a Roger Daltrey," said Dave Gilmour in retrospect. "All we had was a bass player that would stomp around scowling and making faces."

Pink Floyd also withdrew from the pop singles game. The last Barrett-penned seven-inch, "Apples and Oranges," hadn't fared very well on the charts. Two subsequent singles—Wright's "It Would Be So Nice" and Waters' "Point Me at the Sky"—had met with even less success. After that, Pink Floyd simply stopped releasing singles. At the time, this was an unprecedented move. But it was one of the factors that helped establish the album rock format that would come to rule the Seventies. For better or worse, one outcome of the late Sixties' counterculture upheaval is that rock music came to be regarded as serious art. It was no longer about "cute" lead singers and disposable pop singles. In the wake of early concept albums like *Freak Out* by the Mothers of Invention and the Beatles' *Sgt. Pepper's Lonely Hearts Club Band*, groups were emboldened to take the entire 45 minutes or so of a 33 rpm, long-playing vinyl disc as their canvas, converting the album from a collection of isolated songs to a unified single work.

Pink Floyd applied this concept not only to album recordings but also to live performances. By 1969 they were structuring their concerts as two extended song cycles called The Man and The Journey—a "day in the life" concept that included pieces of stage business such as a tea break.

"There was a lovely bit in the show," Waters later recalled, "where we would put a radio on the stage, tune it to a local station and put a mic in front of it, so it was going out the P.A. And we'd stop and make a cup of tea. Just leave the radio playing, make the tea and drink it. And 10 minutes later, or whatever, we'd put the tea cups away, turn the radio off and get on with the music. There were these magical moments of small rock theatre that I loved."

Pink Floyd broadened their reputation as creators of large-scale musical works by writing and recording the soundtrack to Barbet Schroeder's 1969 feature film *More*. They had earlier contributed songs to the youth cult film *Tonite Let's All Make Love in London*. But this was something more grandiose—a full-on film score, albeit a rather song-oriented one. The group also collaborated with director Michelangelo Antonioni on music for the celebrated Italian director's counterculture film *Zabriskie Point*. Waters collaborated with the band's longtime friend and golf partner Ron Geesin on music for another film, *The Body*.

Pink Floyd's emphasis on live performance and their penchant for really big works were reflected on their next album release. Released in late 1969, *Ummagumma* is a double-album set. One album consists of live performances; the other is made up of solo works, two per side, by each of the four band members. One of the high points of the live material is a cacophonous extended version of "Careful with That Axe, Eugene," originally the B side of the aforementioned "Point Me at the Sky."

By this point, psychedelia was starting to wane, but pieces like "Eugene" helped contextualize Pink Floyd within the art rock scene that got underway in the early Seventies. The atonal and aleatoric aspects of the band's live improvisation had always been slightly at odds with the more blissful, raga-based cadences of much psychedelic guitar rock anyway. But it slotted in nicely amid art rock acts like Can, Van Der Graaf Generator or even King Crimson.

Equally artsy, although in another way, is *Atom Heart Mother*, released in October 1970. The title track is a protracted instrumental with fairly elaborate orchestral and choral overdubs written and conducted by the aforementioned Ron Geesin. Waters, Wright and Gilmour contribute one understated acoustic-based piece each. And the album concludes with the pastoral, three-part, group written instrumental "Alan's Psychedelic Breakfast," complete with the sound of frying eggs, radio broadcasts, toilet flushes and other auditory effects associated with the morning.

As had been the case ever since *Saucerful of Secrets*, the album graphics were created by the graphic design firm Hipgnosis, headed by the band's old Cambridge pal Storm Thorgerson. The album's cover shot of a lone cow complements the pastoral mood of much of the music. But the artwork contains no photos of the band—one more step away from the cult of personality and the usual iconography of rock stardom. Apart from its aesthetic interest, this de-emphasis of personal appearance has contributed greatly to the Floyd's ability to continue their careers far past the usual age of rock stars.

Whatever fascination *Ummagumma, Atom Heart Mother* and *More* may hold for diehard Floyd fans, not one of them is an actual, full-on, rock band studio album. (One is a live album combined with solo studio tracks, another is an orchestral lark and the third is a film score.) While consolidating much of their live approach and visual aesthetic during the 1968–71 period, the group was clearly groping for a coherent musical direction. In retrospect, Dave Gilmour has gone so far as to denounce *Atom Heart Mother* as "a load of rubbish. We were at a real down point. We didn't know what on earth we were doing or trying to do at the time, none of us. We were really out there. I think we were scraping the barrel a bit at that period."

The group finally began to find its feet on 1971's *Meddle* album, although this project too began in a bit of a muddle. When the members of Pink Floyd assembled in Abbey Road Studios in January

Guitarist David Gilmour (*left*) joined Pink Floyd in 1968. Briefly a five-member band, they lost Syd Barrett shortly thereafter. *Continuing right*: Nick Mason, Rick Wright, Roger Waters.

1971, they had no material. Nothing had been written in advance. But as they'd done in the past, they began to develop material on the spot. In the process they amassed some 36 musical segments of varying lengths. These fragmentary bits were then assembled into a meaningful sequence after the fact. The result was "Echoes." It took up one entire side of the original vinyl release. Described by Roger Waters as an "epic sound poem," "Echoes" proved to be a pivotal track for Pink Floyd, one that foreshadowed the sound that would conquer AOR radio in the mid Seventies.

The flip side of the original vinyl LP also continued one of the first Pink Floyd tracks that actually did become ubiquitous on AOR radio. "One of These Days (I'm Going to Cut You into Little Pieces)" is built around a Roger Waters bass figure, processed through an echo unit to give it a propulsive, bolero-esque rhythm. Atmospheric sounds and dramatic organ stabs weave rollercoaster dynamics around the hypnotic bass pulse. Pink Floyd had abandoned the pop singles market shortly after Syd Barrett's departure. But with "One of These Days" they'd found a musical form that slotted perfectly into the new album rock radio format that had sprung up in the wake of late-Sixties freeform FM radio.

Eschewing the three-minute, quick-fix mentality of pop radio, AOR purported to provide listeners with a more profound musical experience by playing tracks from albums other than any singles culled from them. This was meant to favor the longer, more instrumental-based styles of music that the hippie/psychedelic thing had brought into vogue. Tracks like "One of These Days" beautifully satisfied the need for this "deeper" kind of radio content, while still managing to be quite hooky. "Progressive" rock notwithstanding, human beings have been suckers for a musical hook since the dawn of time. Pink Floyd were well on their way to a new incarnation as AOR hitmakers.

But there was one more side trip along the way. Shortly after *Meddle* was completed, Pink Floyd did another film score for *More* director Barbet Schroeder. This one was for his film *La Vallée*, although the band's soundtrack ended up being released under the title *Obscured by Clouds*. The score was knocked off in a week, but it yielded one track that would be prophetic of things to come. Waters' composition "Free Four" is a succinct early statement of the grim world view that would become Waters' primary lyrical theme. In it, an aged and dying man looks back on a life that seems short and futile. This would hardly be the first time that Waters would attempt to encapsulate in musical form an entire lifespan filled with frustration and anxiety.

CHAPTER THREE: *DARK SIDE OF THE MOON*

As these words are being written, "Money," "Brain Damage," "Us and Them" or some other song from *Dark Side of the Moon* is being broadcast by a classic rock station nearby. In fact, classic rock radio listeners all across the United States will have heard one of these songs today. Twenty-five years before the day this was written, those who tuned in to classic rock radio inevitably heard one of these songs. Twenty-five years from now, this will probably still be the case. And if some student of ancient history should read these words a few centuries from now, he or she will probably be familiar with these songs. Given the tenacity of classic rock radio, that will probably still be around too.

No account of *Dark Side of the Moon* can fully explain the record's phenomenal sales performance. It spent some 14 years atop various

Billboard charts. At one point, there was rumored to be a CD factory in Germany devoted exclusively to turning out copies of *Dark Side of the Moon*, in a Wagnerian effort to supply worldwide demand for this 1973 rock album.

Dark Side is the work of a seasoned rock band finding itself for the second time—and discovering itself to be more stable and competent than ever before. It was a reflection of all that had come before, and yet it was completely new. By 1972, when work began on the album, David Gilmour had fully defined his role within Pink Floyd and was confident within that role—perhaps for the first time since taking over from Syd Barrett in 1968. And Roger Waters had now found his lyrical voice and his grand theme. For the first time in Pink Floyd's recording career, Waters was the sole lyricist on *Dark Side*.

Songwriting sessions for the album commenced in a warehouse in Bermondsey in London. "When we started, we just discussed the barest outline of what we were going to do," Gilmour would recall. "Then Roger Waters would come into the warehouse every day with bits and pieces of lyrics, and we all added music to them."

This was a far cry from making it up in the studio, as Pink Floyd had often done in the past. The group even played the *Dark Side of the Moon* material live in concert over a period of four months to work out any rough spots before entering Abbey Road Studios on June 1 to begin recording the album. Pink Floyd had used 16-track technology for the first time on *Meddle*. *Dark Side* was their first full-blown 24-track recording.

The album would turn out to be an audio tour de force. It was engineered by Alan Parsons, who had been an apprentice engineer on the Beatles' *Abbey Road* sessions and would go on to a productive solo career as a purveyor of high-fidelity FM radio ear candy. *Dark Side of the Moon* was originally recorded with a view to accommodating "quadraphonic" sound—a four-speaker playback format that was touted at the time as the next big thing in consumer audio. (Much like 5.1 today, albeit with far less Orwellian marketing forces behind it.) The result is a work of cinemascopic proportions, one which draws on all the aural resources of cinematic narrative: words, music and sound effects.

Waters' storyline is, quite simply, one human lifespan—much the same subject as "Free Four" from *Obscured by Clouds*, only now extended to an epic album-length journey. (A format perhaps better suited to so large a topic.) Lyrically, Waters' structure for the album is quite minimal. It revolves around four themes, each of which has its own song: "Time," "Money," War ("Us and Them") and Madness ("Brain Damage.") Human life, in Waters' view, is basically a race against time. Time seems plentiful in youth, but with maturity comes the awareness that time is running out. The majority of adult life is spent "on the run." To dramatize this theme, Waters uses the age-old imagery of the daily cycle—the sun and the moon.

> "And you run and you run to catch up with the sun,
> but it's sinking
> And racing around to come up behind you again.
> The sun is the same in the relative way, but you're older,
> Shorter of breath and one day closer to death."
> ("Time")

Time, says the ancient adage, is money. And a tragically large portion of the short human lifespan is spent in pursuit of money—a state of affairs Waters explores in the sardonic song that is by far *Dark Side*'s greatest hit, and quite possibly the best-known number in the entire Pink Floyd canon. Unlike its namesake, which is often hard to come by, the song "Money" materialized quite effortlessly, according to Nick Mason: "When Roger wrote ['Money'], it more or less all came up in the first day." The song's distinctive 7/8 time signature proved a creative catalyst.

"It was just a tune around those sevenths," Waters told the press. "And I knew there had to be a song about money in the piece. Having decided that, it was extremely easy to make up a seven-beat intro that went with it. I often think that the best ideas are the most obvious ones, and that's a fantastically obvious thing to do, and that's why it sounds good."

Money, says Waters and an old proverb, is the root of all evil. And there is perhaps no greater evil than war. "Us and Them" is sung from the perspective of ordinary, decent men ordered to kill and die by generals who sit safely at the rear of the battle. The song touches on the subject perhaps closest to Waters' heart: the loss of his father in WWII. In "Us and Them," Waters points out that money—the economic interests of the privileged class—is the cause of most wars:

> "With, without
> And who'll deny it's what the fighting's all about?"

So, human life is short and brutal. We're compelled to spend most of it in the consciousness-numbing pursuit of money just to sustain this brief, miserable existence. And there's a strong likelihood that it will be cut short anyway, by war or some other calamity. Confronted with all this, what does a sensitive, thoughtful young man do? He goes mad. Mad like Syd did. And in the song "Brain Damage" Waters imagines himself inside Syd's madness. ("The lunatic is in my head...") Waters appropriates Syd's insanity as the inevitable outcome of his own grim conclusions about life. He finds himself in agreement with the ancient philosopher who pondered the adversities and absurdities of life and decided that the only sane conclusion is to go insane—to take up residence on the dark side of moon, the side that faces away from the sun.

The moon has always been a slippery, ambiguous symbol in Western art. And *Dark Side of the Moon* is no exception. As much as it seems to represent a withdrawal into madness, the moon also seems to suggest a retreat into the inner world of the imagination. Creativity is another reaction to the apparent futility of life. But as the members of Pink Floyd all knew from living with Syd Barrett, the line between creativity and insanity is a very fine one indeed.

"The dark side of the moon itself is an allusion to the moon and lunacy," Dave Gilmour once (somewhat tautologically) observed. "The dark side is generally related to what goes on inside people's heads, the subconscious and the unknown."

The moon image returns at the end of the album's closing track, "Eclipse," a grand, sweeping piece of music that tells us we are all we experience in the course of a lifetime. ("All that you touch, all that you see, all that you taste...") And weighed in the balance— Waters' balance, anyway—it all comes out more dark than light.

> "And everything under the sun is in tune
> But the sun is eclipsed by the moon."

Some four years earlier, in the same recording studio, the Beatles had concluded their masterful *Abbey Road* album with the line, "And in the end the love you take is equal to the love you make." Waters might be inclined to substitute the word "shit" for "love" in the grimmer vision that informs *Dark Side of the Moon*, and indeed much of his work. The universality of *Dark Side*'s themes is undoubtedly one factor in the album's enduring popularity. They reflect the feelings and concerns of many in early adulthood. Today's nu-metal acts state many of these same dark conclusions about the human condition far more bluntly. Waters may not go so far as to join Slipknot in asserting that "People = Shit." But the evidence he presents in works like *Dark Side of the Moon* and *The Wall* certainly does nothing to invalidate that equation.

The power of Waters' lyrics for *Dark Side* lies as much in what he doesn't say as what he does. He sketches the outlines of his course-of-a-lifetime narrative and then leaves the music and sound effects to fill in the tale—or rather to inspire the listener to do so in his or her own terms. *Dark Side of the Moon* is rich in evocative instrumental passages. One recurring motif—a slow, almost Neil Young-ish, Im7-IV progression first introduced in the instrumental "The Great Gig in the Sky"— provides an ideal solo vehicle for both Gilmour and Wright.

Much of the music drifts along at a somnambulistic pace, creating a mood of dreamlike detachment. While "Us and Them" is a song about war, the music is anything but violent, strident or cacophonous. Instead, the vocal is wafted on echoey billows of sound—oddly peaceful—as though we were viewing the horrors and folly of human behavior from somewhere up in the clouds. The sedated quality that infuses much of *Dark Side*'s music suggests the catatonic withdrawal of the insane: the eerie inner peace of someone who is beyond feeling, who has severed himself from the disturbing events of life.

Cynics might also detect a note of Waters' much-vaunted arrogance in this mood of detachment—the cold emotional disengagement of one who takes the moral high ground. Fans, on the other hand, might perceive a dispassionate, contemplative, almost Buddhistic take on life. (The first sound heard on the album is a human heartbeat, and the first word sung is an invitation to breathe. Meditation also begins by focusing on the breath and heartbeat.) The curious discontinuity between the pessimism of the album's lyrics and the tranquillity of the music helps make *Dark Side* a fascinatingly multifaceted work. It is an album that invites repeated listenings and can support multiple interpretations.

However intriguing on a conceptual level, this discontinuity between music and lyrics arises from the simple, pragmatic fact that these two elements originated from different sources on *Dark Side* and subsequent Floyd albums. From this disc on, lyrics would be almost exclusively Waters' domain, while Gilmour and Wright were increasingly in charge of the music. This would eventually lead to substantially different conceptions of Pink Floyd on the part of Waters and Gilmour—a rift that would escalate into violent dispute. Toward the end of the *Dark Side* sessions, Waters and Gilmour had a difference of opinion over the mix, which led to Chris Thomas being called in to complete mixing for the project. Some of the comments Gilmour made around the time of *Dark Side*'s release hint at greater tensions to come.

"For Roger Waters it is more important to do things that say something," Gilmour told one journalist. "Richard Wright is more into putting out good music. And I'm in the middle with Nick. I want to do it all, but sometimes I think Roger can feel the musical content is less important and can slide around it."

Along with lyrics and music, the abundant sound effects on *Dark Side of the Moon* play a huge role in creating mood and conveying a sense of narrative—of real-life events unfolding. Pink Floyd had incorporated the sounds of everyday life into their music from the very beginning—from the tinkling bell in "Bike" on *Piper at the Gates of Dawn*, to the use of random radio broadcasts in concert, to the full blown effects track on "Alan's Psychedelic Breakfast." But with *Dark Side*, Pink Floyd reached a new level of sophistication in incorporating sound effects into their music. Much of this was the work of Nick Mason, operating either on his own or in tandem with Roger Waters. The two had long formed a clique of sorts within Pink Floyd. They had been drinking buddies back in the days when Syd Barrett and Rick Wright were more interested in psychedelic drugs. In the post-Syd Floyd, Waters and Mason often focused jointly on the conceptual side of album projects, while Gilmour and Wright got on with the music.

" 'Alan's Psychedelic Breakfast' is interesting," Mason stated in one interview, "insofar as although we've all agreed that the piece didn't work, in some ways the sound effects are the strongest part." To which Waters added, "I think the simplest things are often the best. For example, just the sound of the wind at the beginning of

'Cut You into Little Pieces' is bloody effective."

As already mentioned, the first sound heard on *Dark Side of the Moon* is a sound effect—a human heartbeat. "The heartbeat," Gilmour once commented, "alludes to the human condition and sets the mood for the music, which describes the emotions experienced during a lifetime."

Sounds tell a lot of the story in *Dark Side of the Moon*. They're deeply woven into the fabric of the album. The crass *ka-ching* of cash registers becomes part of the actual rhythm track for "Money," evoking the mechanized, relentless march of capitalism. The sound of running footsteps recurs at several points, suggesting the individual's reluctant yet desperate participation in the "rat race." The chiming clocks at the outset of "Time" drive the point home. Throughout the album, snippets of spoken dialogue bubble up from the mix. These come from interviews that Mason and Waters conducted and recorded with everyone from Abbey Road doorman Jerry Driscoll to roadies Pete Watts and Roger the Hat to Wings' guitarist Henry McCulloch. The lively, documentary-style remarks add drama to the fadeouts of "Money" and "Us and Them." *Dark Side of the Moon* is a work filled with effortless and thought-provoking segues, both musical and conceptual.

Released in March 1973, *Dark Side of the Moon* became an integral part of the early Seventies Zeitgeist—a time when bongs, stereo headphones and planetarium laser rock shows were all brand new diversions for post-hippie suburban hedonists. A vinyl copy of *Dark Side*—or, better yet, an eight-track cassette—may well be an indispensable Seventies kitsch accessory. But when the music is played today, as it so often is, it doesn't really come off as nostalgia or camp. Nearly 30 years after its initial release, this eerily tranquil rock album still has the power to mirror whatever emotions, mental constructs and interpretations subsequent generations of listeners bring to it.

CHAPTER FOUR: *WISH YOU WERE HERE*

"There was a time after *Dark Side* where [Pink Floyd] might easily have broken up," Nick Mason once confided to a journalist. "We'd reached all the goals rock bands tend to aim for. Perhaps we were nervous about carrying on—the problems of making a follow-up."

The privileges and the pressures of success both loomed large for Pink Floyd in 1974. On the one hand, they were basking in the glow of *Dark Side*'s immense popularity. In the wake of the album's stellar sales, the band had signed a lucrative new contract with Columbia Records. Columbia chief Clive Davis had lured them away from Capitol with a hefty advance. Life was good.

On the other hand, a lot was riding on the album that Waters, Gilmour, Mason and Wright would come up with as a successor to *Dark Side*. At first, understandably perhaps, they prevaricated. Band members indulged in various solo projects. Then there was an aborted attempt to make an album called *Household Objects*, on which all sounds were to be generated by everyday items such as wine bottles, rubber bands and aerosol spray cans. This intriguing concept was abandoned after three tracks were completed. Around the same time, the band instituted a longstanding media blackout, denying all but a very select few interview requests.

Finally, in rehearsals for a '74 tour, new musical ideas began to emerge. They took the form of three meandering compositions that would provide the starting point for the next two Pink Floyd albums. One of these became "Shine On You Crazy Diamond," the lead track for *Wish You Were Here*. Two other numbers, titled "Raving and Drooling" and "You Gotta Be Crazy" at the time, would surface, much altered, as "Sheep" and "Dogs" on *Animals*.

The band buckled down to work at Abbey Road during the first week of 1975. But by most accounts, the sessions for *Wish You Were Here* were not entirely pleasant. Both Waters and Mason were going through strained marital relations that would end in divorce. Waters' estrangement from his wife Judy provided him with plenty of embittered material that would ultimately form part of *The Wall*. Mason's domestic difficulties tended to render him listless and depressed in the studio, which brought him into conflict with Gilmour, who felt the drummer wasn't pulling his musical weight.

"I really did find time in the studio extremely horrible," Mason later commented.

Gilmour and Waters clashed as well. The guitarist was in favor of including "Shine On You Crazy Diamond," "Raving and Drooling" and "You Gotta Be Crazy" on the album that would become *Wish You Were Here*. But Waters had a different idea. He took "Shine On You Crazy Diamond" and built a concept for the new album around it. Once again, the focal point was Syd Barrett. On *Dark Side*, Syd had figured as a kind of martyr to the ugliness and brutality of modern life. On *Wish You Were Here*, Syd becomes a martyr to the ugliness and brutality of the music biz. Syd's crack-up had occurred in the very first flush of success for Pink Floyd. Now Waters was making artistic use of that crack-up to mirror his own discomfort and misgivings over rock stardom.

"Syd is one of the forerunners of life in the West today," Waters once remarked.

Reflecting its origin in live performance, "Shine On You Crazy Diamond" starts with an extended seven-minutes-plus instrumental preamble, which finds Gilmour in a plaintive, bluesy guitar vein that is well suited to Waters' dark lyrical content. (Waters would later complain of "the very drawn out nature of the overture bits that go on and on and on.") When the vocal arrives, we're on familiar ground. Not only is Syd once again fondly recalled as a mad visionary who has moved on to some strange quasi-mystical headspace, the lyrics also employ much of the same dark/light, moon/sun imagery as *Dark Side of the Moon*. To clinch the deal, Dick Parry, who'd played saxophone on "Money," returns to lend his signature stylings to "Shine On You Crazy Diamond." Whether all this represents a deliberate effort to repeat the successful formula of *Dark Side*, an inability to come up with any new ideas or an attempt to create thematic unity from one album to the next is a question open to debate.

The opening track gives way to "Welcome to the Machine," one of the most darkly effective tracks in the entire Floyd canon. The song's funereal, octave vocals and the mechanistic effects Waters coaxes from a VCS3 synthesizer chillingly evoke the zombie clockworks of a cynical and crass music industry. Gilmour's crystalline acoustic guitar shimmers like a dove trying to fly free of the song's infernal landscape. "Welcome to the Machine" and the song that follows it, "Have a Cigar," are quasi-demonic greetings sung in the voice of a sleazy record exec, welcoming a newly arrived rock star (Waters himself, presumably) to the grim world of profits and sales charts. Our hero's naive dreams of "driving Jaguars and eating in the Steak Bar" have entrapped him in something distinctly unsavory—something he couldn't have foreseen.

"The Machine is self-perpetuating," Waters has said, "because its fuel consists of dreams. The rock machine isn't oiled and doesn't actually run on people's appreciation of music, or their wish to interest themselves in music and listen to it, in my opinion. At the base of it all, it runs on dreams. It's for that reason that people throw themselves into it, not to make music … And the dream is that when you are successful, when you're a star, you'll be fine. Everything will go wonderfully well. That's the dream, and as everybody knows, it's an empty one."

The title track, "Wish You Were Here," once again evokes Syd Barrett, with whom Waters seems to emphasize more than ever, over the distance of years. "We're just two lost souls swimming in a fish bowl," sings Waters, "year after year. Running over the same old ground." But it's not exactly clear why Waters wishes his former bandmate were there. To commiserate with him in his disillusionment? To help the band out of their creative lethargy with some new song ideas?

"It could equally have been called *Wish We Were Here*," Waters once quipped, in reference to the many uninspired moments the band spent in the studio.

The album closes with a reprise of "Shine On You Crazy Diamond," thus recapitulating *Dark Side*'s device of ending with the beginning. Commercially, *Wish You Were Here* was a resounding success and continues to be an enduring favorite with many Floyd fans. It offers many of the same pleasures as *Dark Side of the Moon*— plush stereophonics, solid instrumental improvisation, a conceptual framework and some memorable songs. But these elements never quite gel as effectively as they did on *Dark Side*. Many aspects of the work—the use of sound effects, for instance—seem more pro forma gestures than moments of true inspiration. On close inspection, *Wish You Were Here* seems all too realistic a reflection of the doubts and insecurities that follow in the wake of stardom.

The history of the album's making and public unveiling seem fraught with oddly portentous little moments. Like the appearance of the real Syd Barrett—overweight and dressed in a shabby raincoat— at the mixing session for "Shine On You Crazy Diamond." As the song played back over the monitors, lyrics loudly celebrating Waters' idealized "martyr, legend and seer of visions," the semicoherent, flesh-and-blood Barrett proceeded to spook most of those present and put a damper on a celebration in honor of David Gilmour's wedding, held at the studio canteen. He then disappeared, as mysteriously as he'd turned up, never to be seen by the band again.

Perhaps he was present in spirit at the concert premiere of *Wish You Were Here* on July 5, 1975, at an outdoor festival in Knebworth. Or maybe he'd sent some invisible gremlins to gum up the works. Pink Floyd's staging and props had grown increasingly more elaborate over the years. One of the attractions laid on for that show was two WWII Spitfire airplanes. (Some kind of homage, conscious or unconscious, to Waters' slain father?) They were scheduled to fly low over the crowd at the outset of the Floyd's set. In their efforts to time the first notes of their performance to the passing of the aircraft, the band ran afoul of some power generators, with the result that Rick Wright's keyboards were horribly out of tune as he sounded the first notes of "Shine On You Crazy Diamond." In the wake of this inauspicious beginning, the first half of the set went disastrously. Meanwhile, backstage, veteran rocker Roy Harper, who had sung the lead vocal to "Have a Cigar" on the album, was set to reprise his performance live at the concert. But when he was unable to locate his stage clothing, he threw a violent tantrum, destroying one of Pink Floyd's vans in the process and doing some damage to himself as well. Pink Floyd wouldn't give another live performance for the next two years.

CHAPTER FIVE: *ANIMALS*

The Battersea power station is a familiar sight to jet-lagged London visitors who arrive via the Gatwick Express. It stands alongside the river Thames facing north—a massive, grimy edifice, architecturally unremarkable, ugly even. Four immense, dingy white towers rise from the corners of the structure, pushing rudely skyward. Even if you know nothing of the building, you can sense it has something to do with power. When you see it, you know you're in London.

But the Battersea power station is also familiar to legions of rock fans who have never been near Britain's capital city. It is, of course, the building that graces the cover of Pink Floyd's 1977 album, *Animals*. This stark, arresting cover image (again the work of the band's old Cambridge pal, Storm Thorgerson, and his groundbreaking design firm, Hipgnosis) is a landmark in Pink Floyd history. It served notice to 1977 record buyers that a new mood had come to Pink Floyd, and indeed to England. Gone are the fanciful, surreal graphics of former Floyd discs. Here is a very real, industrialized landscape, photographed beneath a lowering London sky. (Only on closer inspection does one realize that there is a slightly stylized, inflated rubber pig floating between two of the power plant's massive stacks.) The inside of the original 12-inch vinyl gatefold sleeve offered further images of urban blight—barbed wire, broken windows, train tracks—photographed in and around Battersea in gloomy black and white.

The sound of *Animals* matches the cover graphics. It's nowhere near as plummy as *Dark Side of the Moon* or *Wish You Were Here*. The music is still as ambitious as ever: rock compositions in multiple parts with conceptual lyrics and plenty of room for improvisation. But the sonic texture has toughened appreciably. While this development may have come as bad news for some of the headphones and hash pipe set, it was welcomed by many who were attuned to where rock was going in the late Seventies.

There are several theories that account for *Animals'* stripped-down sound. One is that punk rock, itself a product of Britain's depressed mid-Seventies economy, was nipping at the Floyd's heels. This may have provided some impetus, either conscious or unconscious, for the band to move toward a more aggressive, less "fat" approach. Secondly, *Animals* was the first album that the band recorded in their then-new studio Britannia Row. In 1976, Pink Floyd began to build a professional studio inside the converted chapel in London's Islington that had formerly been the band's equipment storage, office and rehearsal space, with a modest demo studio on the premises. In time Britannia Row would become a world-class recording facility. But in '76, when *Animals* was recorded, the bugs were still being worked out, which may also account, in part, for the disc's stripped-down sound.

Inter-band relations, which had become strained during the making of *Dark Side* and *Wish You Were Here*, grew even chillier. "That was the first one I didn't write anything for," Rick Wright recalled of *Animals*. "And it was the first album, for me, where the group was losing its unity as well. That was the beginning of where Roger wanted to do everything."

Perhaps Wright's anger at being excluded from the writing got funneled into his snarling Hammond organ work on the album, some of the most fiery playing he has ever done. Indeed, while perhaps still tepid by punk rock standards, many of the album's studio performances have a scrappy, feisty quality. Pink Floyd's music had finally come fully in sync with Waters' aggrieved lyrical stance. As it turned out, this would be the last Pink Floyd disc where the classic Waters/Wright/Gilmour/Mason lineup would be heard playing together, all on their own.

Animals grew out of two pieces, "You Gotta Be Crazy" and "Raving and Drooling," that Pink Floyd had written back in 1974 and developed in live performance. From this material, Waters developed a concept as engaging in its structural simplicity as the Time/Money/War/Madness theme he created for *Dark Side of the Moon*. With obvious indebtedness to George Orwell's social allegorical novel *Animal Farm*, Waters' *Animals* reduces all human society to three categories. There are the pigs: the ruling class, politicians, bosses, oppressors—both economic and moral—censors, the self-righteous and self-satisfied. The great majority, however, are sheep: those who meekly, blindly and obediently go along with society's program, even though it is a program that is ultimately pernicious for them. Thirdly, there are the dogs: the ruthlessly grasping, the unscrupulous and streetwise, the venture capitalists and business sharpies, crooks in possession of "a club tie and a firm handshake."

"The 'Animals' concept didn't come up until the album was about three-quarters finished," David Gilmour later recalled. "I don't think Roger had it in his mind before, but at some point he realized how close the lyrics were on those tracks and he changed the lyrics about a bit on 'Dogs,' which was called 'You Gotta Be Crazy' before that, and 'Sheep,' which was 'Raving and Drooling' before then. It all obviously fitted together in his mind, coming to mean that. It is a good thing, in the end, having come to a collective decision, though. It knocks out some of the excesses which might otherwise appear from us as individuals."

"Dogs," which takes up most of side one of the album's original vinyl release format, is at heart a cautionary moral tale. The song's canine protagonist pays a steep price for his well-cultivated ability to swindle, deceive and "pick out the easy meat with [his] eyes closed." In so doing, he isolates himself from the rest of humanity.

David Gilmour in 1975.

Larry Hulst/Retna

He becomes "only a stranger at home," and in the end dies of cancer, sad and alone. The lyrical passages in the song are interspersed with stately harmonized guitar interludes from Gilmour, which rank as some of the most majestic stuff amid all the pomp and circumstance that is Seventies rock.

Side two begins with "Pigs (Three Different Ones)," which skewers porcine behavior, devoting one verse to a real-life figure, Mary Whitehouse. Britain's arbiter of decency—a one-woman equivalent of the PMRC or Christian Coalition in the U.S.—Whitehouse had targeted Pink Floyd as early as 1967 for advocating drug use in their music.

Next comes "Sheep," in which Waters espouses the Marxist view of organized religion as the opiate of the people. As the song's woolly protagonists are led to the slaughter, they chant a vocoder-processed lampoon of the 23rd Psalm:

> "The Lord is my shepherd, I shall not want...
> He maketh me to hang on hooks in high places.
> He converteth me to lamb cutlets..."

As is the case with most rock concept albums, the denouement is a bit muddled. The sheep rebel, apparently, but the revolution fails. The dogs all get killed. (Had they thrown in their lot with the sheep against the pigs? Had the sheep been rebelling against them?) The sheep ultimately decide it's better to stay at home and do as they're told after all. Presumably, the pigs prevail.

Pig, sheep or dog—which are you, then? Waters' societal schema doesn't afford an attractive option. Perhaps to soften the harshness of this outlook, the album is bracketed by a brief prelude and coda ("Pigs on the Wing") in which Waters suggests, to strummed acoustic guitar accompaniment, that his narrative perspective is, ultimately, compassionate. His opening salvo, "If you didn't care what happened to me, and I didn't care for you," gives way to a more matey mood at the end: "You know that I care what happens to you. And I know that you care for me." We are all united, apparently, by our common need to steer clear of pigs on the wing.

With *Animals*, Pink Floyd finally escaped the space rock/sci-fi tag that had stuck with them, much to Waters' chagrin, ever since their early, psychedelic phase. There was nothing here that could remotely be construed as otherworldly. Significantly enough,

Animals is the first Pink Floyd album since *Obscured by Clouds* that doesn't contain a song about Syd. *Animals* consolidated a new, darker mood in Pink Floyd's work—more realistic and more vitriolic than anything that had come before.

But Roger Waters still had more angst that needed to be melded into high-concept rock music.

CHAPTER SIX:
"ROCK'S BIGGEST ERECTION": *THE WALL*

"I actually still have the drawing at home," says Roger Waters, recalling the first of countless sketches he made for Pink Floyd's opus, *The Wall*. The idea came to Waters in 1977. "Sitting on a plane or in a bar somewhere," he remembers, "I got a piece of paper and drew a picture of this wall [running] across an arena, with a stage. When I did that I got very excited; I thought, Wow, what a great piece of theatre it would be to do that—actually to construct a wall between the band and audience during a concert."

Waters' concept turned out to be much more than an interesting piece of rock theater. *The Wall* is the third biggest selling album of all time. It spawned one of the largest, most elaborate stage productions ever mounted in rock—so large, in fact, that the show could only run for a handful of performances in four cities and all but bankrupted the band in the process. Waters' protean brainchild was also made into a motion picture in 1982 with rock star and future philanthropist Bob Geldof in the lead role.

The Wall's influence continues to be felt in current rock. Nine Inch Nails mastermind Trent Reznor has taken many a cue from Waters' dark themes of downward spiraling rock-star psychosis, and is an avid collector of animation stills from the '82 film version of *The Wall*. Present-day angst rockers like Marilyn Manson and Korn also owe a considerable debt to Waters' and Pink Floyd's strident masterwork.

What Shall We Do Now?

By the late Seventies, Pink Floyd had been through more than a decade's worth of trials and triumphs and were on the verge of collapse from within. Over the years, Roger Waters had come into his own as Pink Floyd's major thinker. But his ascendancy had created no small amount of bad feeling between himself and his bandmates, who tended to view the bassist as an increasingly tyrannical control freak. Friction between Waters and Gilmour grew particularly intense, as both men vied, in very different ways, to fill Syd Barrett's shoes—Gilmour through guitaristic prowess and melodic songcraft and Waters through boldly experimental concepts. Born in a psychological war zone, *The Wall* strained Pink Floyd to the breaking point. Rick Wright, who had been with Pink Floyd since day one, left the group during the making of *The Wall*, which was also to prove Waters' penultimate project with the band. And for the first time in Pink Floyd history session men were brought in to play instruments, such as drums, that had hitherto always been handled by the core members of the group.

"There's always been tension," Gilmour says of his relationship with Waters. "But it was all quite controllable until after *The Wall* album. There's such a thing as creative tension. And then there's total egocentric, megalomaniac tension, if you like."

Is There Anybody Out There?

There were other tensions in the air at the time of *The Wall*'s creation—tensions within rock music itself. By the late Seventies, the punk rock revolution had heaped much invective on the decade's big stadium rock bands such as Pink Floyd. Punk moved rock music back into small clubs, which permitted a closer connection between bands and their audiences. Punk ideologues honed in on Pink Floyd's inflatable pig prop in particular as a symbol of the bloated, foolish thing corporate rock had become.

What few punk rockers realized at the time is that Roger Waters had come to the exact same conclusion himself. As Pink Floyd had moved from small psychedelic venues like London's UFO club into larger and larger arenas and stadiums, Waters had come to feel increasingly alienated and isolated from concert audiences.

"It was magical in the early days of Floyd," he says. "But the magic was eaten by the numbers. By '77, when we were doing the *Animals* tour—playing only big stadiums and selling out everywhere—all everyone was talking about was grosses and numbers and how many people there were in the house. And you could hardly hear yourself think. You could hardly hear anything [onstage] because there were so many drunk people in the stadium, all shouting and screaming."

The situation reached a crisis point during a Pink Floyd concert at Olympic Stadium in Montreal, where Waters spat at an especially obnoxious fan. Appalled by his own behavior, the bassist began to ponder how things had ever come to such a pass that he could feel actual hostility toward a member of his audience. Shortly after the Montreal incident, Waters came up with the aforementioned drawing of a gigantic wall, a barrier between performers and spectators.

The incredible power of the image Waters chose lies in its simplicity and universality. It is an ancient, quasi-mystical symbol that comes down to us from the dark recesses of biblical and classical antiquity. Writers from Melville to Sartre have used the wall image as a symbol of alienation. It has become particularly identified with the feeling of existentialist isolation unique to the post-WWII era—the latter half of the 20th century. In this epoch, we all live behind walls—political, psychological, social, self-imposed or otherwise. In applying this rich motif to rock—the great late 20th-century populist art form—Waters found the basis for the most ambitious project of his career. In the past, he'd played an important role in creating concept albums for Pink Floyd. But now he envisioned a concept album that would also form the basis for a series of concert performances and a feature film.

"I needed to construct the whole piece," Waters says. "So I started thinking, Well, what is this wall, and what's it made from? Then the idea started to occur to me that the individual bricks might be from different aspects of the history of my life and other people's lives. And I started to fit things together."

Back at his country home, Waters began writing songs for what would become *The Wall*. He put together a demo tape "that was only 43 minutes long, or something like that," he recalls. During the same period he worked up a rough demo for another project, *The Pros and Cons of Hitch Hiking*, which would eventually become his first solo album. Initially, however, both projects were presented to the other members of Pink Floyd. Waters invited them to choose which of the two demos they wanted to make into the next Pink Floyd album. They opted, of course, to do *The Wall*.

At this juncture, the band was on the brink of bankruptcy, owing to some ill-advised business investments. They desperately needed another best-selling Pink Floyd album, on the order of *Dark Side of the Moon* or *Animals*. It has been widely speculated that Pink Floyd might not have stayed together to make *The Wall* had they not been in such dire financial straits. The situation being what it was, Gilmour, Wright and Mason joined forces with Waters to make what would become a fittingly grand last hurrah for Seventies rock, and a record that would set the stage for Waters and the other group members to go their separate ways in the Eighties. It was deemed necessary, however, to bring in an outside producer—rock vet Bob Ezrin—to work on *The Wall*. Ezrin's role in part, was to act as a mediator, particularly between Waters and Gilmour.

"It was, for the most part, a typically British polite enmity that existed between them," Ezrin recollects. "They were obviously close on many levels. And there was an unadmitted mutual respect beneath all the arguing and bickering going on between them. But the tension was always present, because there was a war between two basically dominant personalities. Each one had a need to express himself in his own style. And sometimes these styles were very different. Sometimes they approached the same piece of material from an entirely different point of view. So my job was often to be Henry Kissinger and run back and forth between the two of them, trying to work arrive at a workable middle ground."

Empty Spaces

Perhaps best known, at the time, for his production work with Alice Cooper and Kiss, Ezrin had also produced Peter Gabriel's first solo album (a particular favorite of Waters) and had helped bring Lou Reed's bleak, difficult concept album *Berlin* into being. Before sessions for *The Wall* began, Ezrin spent some time with Waters massaging the plot line. "I went and spent a weekend with him and reviewed his original demo," says the producer. "In there were the germs for I'd say half the songs that ended up appearing on the final album. From that, we refined the plot line and developed a slightly different story from the original one that Roger had. We filled in holes, the way you do with a movie script, and built the album around the story."

One of Ezrin's suggestions was to change *The Wall* from a first-person narrative in Waters' own voice to a third-person story focusing on a character named Pink Floyd. (A throwback to the sleazy record exec in "Have a Cigar" who asks, "Oh, by the way, which one's Pink?" In the band's early career, nightclub managers and other non-hipsters would assume that there was actually a band member named Pink Floyd.) Pink's father, an RAF fighter pilot, dies in WWII when the boy is still in infancy. In the piece, war functions as a metaphor for what corporate rock had, in Waters' view, become. Touring rock bands are like soldiers wearily slogging from one town to the next, "doing their duty" for their corporate superior officers back at record company HQ. The indignities suffered by stadium rock concertgoers—festival seating stampedes, deafening P.A. systems—are likened to the sufferings visited on victims of war. All this might seem a bit of an overexaggeration. Or perhaps not, depending on how many stadium rock concerts one has attended.

As the plot unfolds, we see that smothering, overprotective love from Pink's mother impedes the boy's psychological development. He begins to erect a mental barrier—a wall—between himself and the outside world. As he grows to manhood, he is further traumatized by a sadistic schoolmaster (emblematic of the repressive British public school system) and the infidelity of his wife. Each of these bad experiences is "another brick in the wall," causing Pink to withdraw ever further into himself. All of this doesn't prevent Pink from becoming a rock star, although his rise to fame is not depicted in the story—a curious narrative omission.

By midpoint in the piece (the end of the first disc), Pink has become totally alienated from the outside world. The wall he'd begun erecting in childhood is now complete. Isolated in a solipsistic inner world, he becomes prey to "the worms": his own anxieties, doubts and fears. After receiving an injection to rouse him from his catatonic state so he can perform onstage (the subject matter of "Comfortably Numb"), a strange transformation comes over Pink. He turns into a quasi-Nazi. His concert performance that evening takes the form of a fascist rally, with Pink singling out "queers," Jews and "coons" in the audience, singing "If I had my way, I'd have you all shot" ("In the Flesh").

With this rather strong metaphor, which some have found in questionable taste, Waters is dramatizing the feelings that led him to spit on the audience member at the '77 Montreal show. But if Pink is hard on his fans, he's even harder on himself. The final scenes of The Wall take the form of a trial enacted within Pink's own psyche. A "worm judge" presides. The sadistic schoolmaster and faithless wife return as witnesses who testify against Pink. The verdict is to tear down the wall Pink has built around himself. But the ending is ambiguous. Is the wall's collapse a good thing—a return to reality for the troubled Pink? Or is it a bad thing—a further trauma for the already unbalanced protagonist?

The final lines of the piece sound a note of sympathy for those close to Pink. (The same ones who drove him crazy in the first place?) For them, "it's not always easy banging your heart against some mad bugger's wall" ("Outside the Wall").

As far as plot is concerned, it's hard not to notice *The Wall*'s many similarities to an earlier rock opus, the Who's *Tommy* (1969), which also formed the basis for a double album, a rock concert performance, a film and—years later—a stage play. Tommy, like Pink, has a British fighter pilot for a father, and as *Tommy* opens, we learn that the protagonist's father is missing in action, presumed dead, in the war (WWI in the album version, WWII in the film.) Also like Pink, Tommy withdraws into himself as a result of psychological pressures brought to bear by his mother. Pink becomes a rock star. Tommy becomes a messianic guru, not unlike a rock star. Tommy and Pink both turn authoritarian on their followers toward the end of their respective stories. Pink undergoes an awakening of sorts when a wall is torn down. Tommy undergoes a similar jolt to consciousness when a mirror is smashed.

Waters' plot gets few points, if any, for originality. But what sets *The Wall* apart from *Tommy* is its tone. *Tommy* is much lighter in mood, reflecting the spiritual aspirations of its author, Pete Townshend, as much as his doubts about rock stardom. Pink's alienated psyche is a hellish, worm infested place. Tommy's isolation is "a quiet vibration land," a quasi-meditative state of peace and stillness. The villains in *Tommy*—Cousin Kevin, Uncle Ernie, etc.— are presented with a note of broad, albeit dark, comedy. But there's nothing funny about Pink's tormentors. They have the cruel stench of real human beings. It's no secret that Waters was profoundly influenced by the raw, painfully confessional approach that John Lennon had pursued on his first solo album (*Plastic Ono Band*, 1971). Much like Lennon, Waters was traumatized by the early death of a parent. And unlike Pete Townshend's, Waters' father really did die in the Second World War.

"When I was three or four," Waters recalls, "suddenly there were these men in uniform picking the other kids up from kindergarten. My father was missing in action. So there was always that feeling of 'maybe one day…' You know? I've written lots of poetry about that, apart from all this stuff in *The Wall*. I think that is maybe one of the things that makes people performers. I think it engenders in you a tendency to jump through hoops. 'Maybe if I jump through this hoop, my dad will come back.' I know it sounds crazy. But I really think that.

"A few years ago I had a kind of enlightening moment in my therapeutic process: I suddenly was able to explain dreams that I had had periodically throughout my life. I used to have this very very vivid, recurring dream that I'd murdered somebody and I was going to get caught, get punished, whatever. And I came to realization that, on some subconscious level, I felt that I had killed my father. I was born and he died. I haven't had the dream ever since that realization. So I don't know—maybe that whole experience has provided me with part of whatever it is one needs to empathize. That's partly why a lot of my work focuses on the impotence of the innocent victim."

It is this aspect of *The Wall* that speaks most urgently to the post-grunge generation of rock fans. Korn, for instance, hit a tremendously responsive chord in its young audience by dealing with the early-life psychological traumas and purported childhood abuse of band leader Jonathan Davis. The image of a child's battered cuddly toy used in the cover art for Korn's 1999 album, *Issues*, bears an uncanny resemblance to a similar image that graphic artist Gerald Scarfe created 20 years earlier for *The Wall*'s album jacket and motion picture animation. Consciously or not, Marilyn Manson also seems to borrow heavily from *The Wall* on his *Antichrist Superstar* album. A "worm" motif figures prominently in that work. And its protagonist also develops a Nazi alter ego, just like Pink. In fact, the album's cover photo of Antichrist Superstar in Nazi-style regalia is strikingly similar to the costume, makeup and hairstyle used by Bob Geldof during the "fascist rally" scenes in the film version of *The Wall*.

Bring the Boys Back Home

Around April 1979, members of Pink Floyd did a little recording for *The Wall* at their own studio, Britannia Row, in England. But after a few sessions they were informed by management that, owing to tax issues stemming from their recent financial difficulties, they would have to make the album outside of England. So the quartet moved operations to Superbear studios in France and then completed the album at Producers Workshop in Los Angeles. The album was still only partially written when sessions got underway.

"Some things were kind of complete on the original demo," Waters recalls, "including 'Waiting for the Worms,' 'Mother,' 'Another Brick in the Wall, Parts 1, 2, 3' and 'Is There Anybody out There.' A lot of the stuff obviously developed after that. I remember sitting in a room while the tracks were being recorded and writing 'In the Flesh,' 'Nobody Home' and 'Comfortably Numb.' "

The latter song, one of the best-known and -loved pieces from *The Wall*, marks one of David Gilmour's few songwriting collaborations with Waters on the album. (He also co-wrote "Run Like Hell" and "Young Lust.") "Bob Ezrin's desire was to make *The Wall* a Pink Floyd record rather than Roger's solo record," Gilmour recalls. "Roger wanted it to be all his solo project. He didn't want anyone else to contribute to the writing. But Bob thought there should be other people's writing on the album. So he said to me, 'What have you got?' And I played him my demo for 'Run Like Hell' and what became 'Comfortably Numb.' Bob said, 'Oh, they're really nice. We should include them.' Roger said, 'Well...alright.' It was a long hard process making that record: throwing bits away, tough editing, going to meetings..."

A brilliant evocation of the narcotized, desensitized, late-20th-century consumerist malaise we all live in, "Comfortably Numb" combines the best of Waters' lyrical incisiveness with some of Gilmour's finest music. It is one of several songs on *The Wall* to employ a lush orchestral arrangement, written by Ezrin and Michael Kamen, which further enhances Gilmour's musical themes. Though few in number, Gilmour's songwriting contributions to *The Wall* impart a welcome element of melodicism. They contrast effectively with Waters' own compositions, many of which are sung in a style that Waters developed especially to portray the character Pink—a crabbed, stagily strident set of vocal mannerisms a bit reminiscent of the Kurt Weill/Bertolt Brecht operas of Twenties Berlin. When "Comfortably Numb" comes along, midway through *The Wall*'s second disc, its effect is not unlike that of an operatic aria—a burst of sublime melody that momentarily lifts the listener out of the creaking mechanics of plot development. The chord progression and some melodic elements for "Comfortably Numb" came from a song idea that Gilmour had developed for his first solo album, *David Gilmour* (1978), the guitarist discloses:

"I'd recorded a demo of it when I was at Superbear studios previously, doing my first solo album. We changed the key of the opening section from E to B I think. Then we had to add a couple of extra bars so Roger could do the line, 'I have become comfortably numb.' But other than that, it was very simple to write. And it was all done before the orchestration was added. But there were arguments about how it should be mixed and which backing track should be used. I think it was more of an ego thing than anything else. We actually went head to head over which of two different drum tracks to use. If you put them both on a record today, I don't think anyone could tell the difference. But it seemed important at the time, though. So it ended up with us taking a drum fill out of the one version and putting it into the other version by editing a 16-track tape—splitting it down the middle so you have two strips of tape, 1-inch wide." This is called a window edit.

Tempers flared during the mixdown of "Comfortably Numb" in Los Angeles. A particularly heated confrontation between Gilmour and Waters took place over dinner one night at an Italian restaurant in North Hollywood. "There was no screaming, though," says Ezrin. "It was all very English, very direct: 'You're a fuck and you have no reason to live.' That sort of cold, head-on English confrontation. And I was right in the middle of it. I was fighting at that point for the introduction of the orchestra and the expansion of the Pink Floyd sound into something that was more theatrical, more filmic. But Dave really saw 'Comfortably Numb' more as a bare bones track with just bass, drums and guitar. Roger sided with me on that particular point. What we ended up with is the body of the song being more heavily orchestral, and then the end clears out somewhat and is more rock and roll. So 'Comfortably Numb' is a true collaboration because it's David's music, Roger's lyrics and my orchestral chart!"

Gilmour contributed an especially expressive guitar solo on "Comfortably Numb." Although the solo is beautifully structured, the guitarist says very little forethought, if any, went into it: "As far as I remember, I just went out into the studio at Superbear, banged five or six solos down and then just picked the best bits from each one."

Gilmour vaguely recalls using "a Big Muff with an Electric Mistress flanger" to get his distinctive tone for the solo: "all this stuff going through an amp." Bob Ezrin remembers that they used a Yamaha guitar cabinet with a rotating speaker combined with either a Hiwatt or Marshall amp: "The Yamaha gave it a kind of unearthly quality, which, when added to the basic sound of a distorted, singing Hiwatt, created that beautiful, multitextural guitar sound that you hear at the end of the track. I must say, on that album we probably did every kind of guitar sound known to man, and some that were never done before. One good thing about working with a band like Pink Floyd is their natural inclination toward experimentation. We tried all kinds of new approaches—for that time—to recording. We did a 16-track basic reel and then we had a 24-track slave reel. And then we slaved them together with mini mag a synchronization format that pre-dates SMPTE time code and was quite primitive by comparison. Which was pretty dicey when you look back on it. Kind of like flying without a cockpit."

Waters has fond memories of creating sound effects in the studio. "When we were working at Producers Workshop, all the sound effects and stuff toward the end happened really fast. If we wanted the sound of a smashing TV, we'd buy a TV, go out into the carpark and smash it. I remember the exact car we used for squealing tire effects. It was a station wagon that we had to drive stuff around in. We'd let the air out of the tires, put some water in the parking lot and…screech! We just held a microphone up."

While some of the snippets of film and TV dialogue heard on the album were carefully, and thematically, chosen from English WWII films *The Dambusters* and *The Battle of Britain*, others were left to chance. "Some of it," Waters recalls, "was just, 'I want a bit of TV here. Go turn on the TV in the lounge and put a mic in front of it.' It was just completely random. Whatever was there. It was very exciting to allow things like that to happen."

Other aspects of the project weren't so random. Given their financial predicament, Pink Floyd badly needed a hit single. The group had never really released singles or catered to that market, and were reluctant to do so now. But Bob Ezrin heard considerable melodic potential in "Another Brick in the Wall," a Waters composition that is restated at three different points in the narrative, each time with a different musical arrangement to go with the lyrics. "Another Brick in the Wall, Part 2" contained the memorable lines,

"We don't need no education, we don't need no thought control," but didn't have enough verses to conform to the conventional pop single format. Ezrin had had great success using a children's chorus on Alice Cooper's "School's Out," a song similar in subject matter to "Another Brick Part 2." So word was sent back to Pink Floyd's Britannia Row studios in England. Engineer Nick Griffiths arranged for some children from Islington Green School, just around the corner from Britannia Row, to come into the studio. Griffiths set up some mikes and the children, under the direction of their music teacher, sang the lyric to "Another Brick in the Wall, Part 2," imparting particular gusto to the line, "Hey teacher, leave us kids alone!"

"We were at Producers Workshop at the time," Waters recalls. "I remember sending the multitrack tape to Nick Griffiths in London and asking him to copy the backing track, record the kids, stick it all together and send it back to us. We just had one conversation. The tape came back in a Federal Express parcel, and I remember saying, 'Oh, let's have a listen.' I feel shivery now remembering the feeling of what it was like hearing those kids singing that song. I knew it was a hit record. There were a lot of great moments like that, when we were working at Producers Workshop."

On a less cheerful note, Rick Wright, who'd been with Pink Floyd since the beginning, was dismissed by Waters during the making of *The Wall*. Waters felt the keyboardist wasn't pulling his weight. Bad feelings first arose over Wright's wish to be a producer of the album, along with Waters, Gilmour and Ezrin.

"We agreed at the beginning that if Rick really did help with the production he could then call himself a producer and get credit for it," says Waters. "So Rick would sit in on the sessions from morning 'til night every day and never left the studio. At a certain point, I remember Ezrin getting irritated because Rick said he didn't like some idea. And I remember Ezrin saying about Rick, 'Why does he sit here all day?' "I said, 'Don't you understand? He thinks he's producing the record.' Ezrin said, 'Don't be ridiculous.' To which I replied, 'I promise you. You ask Rick. But wait 'til I'm not here!' He asked him and came back and said, 'You're absolutely right. That's exactly what he thought.' So I said, 'Have you told him?' And he said, 'Yeah. I told him that's not what producing a record is.' So we never saw Rick again. That was it. He disappeared. He got the hump, you know, and that was kind of the beginning of the end, really."

Waters also fell out with graphic designer Storm Thorgerson, who'd been creating Pink Floyd album covers and other artwork for years. Satirical cartoonist Gerald Scarfe wound up collaborating with Waters on the sleeve design for *The Wall*. Scarfe's artwork would become an integral part of the live concert presentation of *The Wall* and the subsequent film as well.

Released on November 20, 1979, *The Wall* was an instant commercial success. But Waters and the surviving members of Pink Floyd had scant leisure to savor their triumph. They plunged almost immediately into the next phase of the project.

In the Flesh

The Wall had initially been conceived as a live performance statement. Before he'd written a note of music or a single scrap of plot, Waters had become obsessed with the powerful visual image of a huge wall stretching across the proscenium of an arena stage. In transforming Pink Floyd's concept double album into a concert spectacle, Waters finally got to build his wall—or rather a full crew of stagehands did, brick by massive cardboard brick, on a nightly basis. The gigantic 130-feet-wide-by-65-feet-high edifice was raised at the lip of the stage as Pink Floyd played the album's music. By the time the colossal edifice was completed, midway through the show, Pink Floyd were completely obscured from the audience's view, hidden behind the wall—an epic-scale enactment of Pink's, and by extension Waters', moment of greatest alienation.

During the second half of the show, the big cardboard wall became the single biggest prop in the entire history of rock and roll. Brick faces swung open to disclose sets and scenes: Pink (played by Waters) sat in his hotel room. Gerald Scarfe's nightmarish animations were projected onto the wall. David Gilmour stood on top of the wall, like the conquering hero in a Hercules movie, to play the "Comfortably Numb" solo. And in the end, of course, the wall came tumbling down, like its biblical predecessor in Jericho.

Everything about the production was big. There was even a "surrogate band": guitarist Snowy White, bassist Andy Bown, drummer Willie Wilson and keyboardist Peter Wood. Intended to represent Pink's band when the protagonist has entered his psychotic fascist alter ego, this quartet came onstage before the actual members of Pink Floyd to play the opening number, "In the Flesh," wearing masks of the four Pink Floyd members' faces. White, Bown, Wilson and Wood then acted as auxiliary musicians throughout the rest of the show. Bown's presence freed Waters from the bass, so he could act out scenes in character, as Pink—albeit with a big pair of headphones on. (This was before the invention of in-ear monitors.) At the time, Waters also groused that Wilson and Wood were necessary because Nick Mason and Rick Wright couldn't play well enough. Although Wright was officially out of Pink Floyd at this point, and had been excluded from the band's business partnership, he did play *The Wall* tour on a salaried basis. Consequently he is the only one of the four who made any money off the tour. The other three sunk their own funds into the enormous production.

And truly enormous it was: 45 tons of equipment and a 45,000-watt P.A. It was quickly determined that many venues just couldn't accommodate so big a show. For a few mad, Spinal Tap moments, the band considered designing and building their own portable concert venue—a kind of high-tech circus tent shaped like a giant slug. Drawings and scale models for this were completed and can be seen in one of the documentary films included in the expanded DVD version of *The Wall*, released in 1999.

Ultimately, however, the "slug" idea was abandoned. Realizing that the show was too big to be a conventional rock tour, Pink Floyd decided to do extended runs at venues in four major cities: the Los Angeles Sports Arena, Nassau Coliseum just outside New York City, Earl's Court in London and Westfallenhalle in Dortmund, West Germany. While all these venues are large arenas, none are the huge sports stadiums that Waters so hated playing, a hatred that moved him to write *The Wall* in the first place.

The scope of the show enabled Waters to include a number of songs he had written for *The Wall* but which didn't make it onto the album. The job of coordinating the live music with all the elaborate staging elements fell to David Gilmour, who was appointed musical director for the show.

"For me *The Wall* show was terrific fun," says the guitarist. "Really an achievement for everyone involved, particularly Roger. But I had to take on the role of music director and deal with a lot of musical details onstage so that Roger didn't have to think about that. It was really tough at first. Later on it got a little easier, once we all got into it. But I had a huge cue sheet up on my amps, because we had all these cues coming up on monitors or on screen, and there were different DDL settings which I had to transmit with very primitive equipment to all the delay lines onstage. Very tricky. Except for the 'Comfortably Numb' solo, there were virtually no moments where I could say, 'Forget everything. Just play.' You know? It was very rigid. Whereas on all the previous tours—*Wish You Were Here, Dark Side of the Moon*—there were moments that could be extended longer or made shorter if you liked. *The Wall*, quite reasonably, because it was a different kind of project, didn't have that."

After a rehearsal in nearby Culver City, the show opened in Los Angeles on February 7, 1980. As if the spectacular effects planned by the show's organizers weren't enough, the opening night audience got a little bonus excitement—a fire onstage early in the performance.

"Andy Bown and Snowy and those guys did their thing," Waters recalls. "And then this drape went up to reveal us. Fireworks had gone off beforehand and one of the roman candles had gotten into this drape and set light to it. I was singing away and I kept hearing this noise and I thought, God, the P.A.'s going off. 'Cause I could hear this strange noise. Eventually I looked up and saw one of the riggers, a guy called Rocky, leap about six feet through the air, with no safety harness or anything on him, from one drape to another. He had a fire extinguisher in one hand and he was trying to put the thing out. And then lumps of burning drape the size of tennis balls started hitting the stage all around us. And the auditorium was beginning to fill up with smoke. I made a decision that this was not cool. So I stopped singing and just shouted 'Stop!' through the P.A. Throughout rehearsals, the guys out at the mixing console were so used to me constantly yelling 'stop'—if something wasn't right, you know. So when I did it during the actual show they must have all thought they were hallucinating. 'Cause they just carried on. So I shouted 'Stop!' again. This time, they said, 'Okay, he really does seem to be saying "stop." I guess we have to.' And I said, 'Look, we're going to have to lower this drape, because we've got a fire. Everything's cool. We'll put it out, go back five minutes and pick up from there.' Which we did. But it was quite a hair-raising beginning to the first show."

The Show Must Go On

The third phase of Waters' original grand conception for *The Wall* was to turn the piece into a full-length motion picture. The idea was to make a film that would rely entirely on the music to tell its story. There was to be no conventional spoken dialogue—a risky and novel concept in the pre-MTV era when the film was in its planning stages. Waters began to turn his attention to a cinematic incarnation of *The Wall* while live performances of the piece were still underway. The original plan was to use footage of *The Wall* live performances in the movie. To that end, five nights at Earl's Court in London were filmed and committed to audiotape.

But the idea of using concert footage in the movie was vehemently opposed by Alan Parker, the man appointed to direct the picture. (Parker's résumé included *Midnight Express* and *Fame* at this point. He would go on to direct the film version of Weber and Rice's *Evita*, with Madonna in the title role.) So the live footage was scrapped, a move that had several ramifications. For one, the Earl's Court material was never seen or heard by the public—until 1999, that is, and the EMI release of *Is There Anybody Out There? The Wall Live* CD. The second ramification is that Roger Waters did not end up playing Pink in the motion picture, as he had done onstage. When the plan was to incorporate elements of the concert in the film, it was a forgone conclusion that Waters would play Pink on screen. The need for continuity pretty much dictated that the same person would have to portray the adult Pink in all scenes. But with the live footage out of the picture, this was no longer an issue. And Waters was persuaded—with some difficulty, apparently—to accept another leading man and indeed not to appear in the film at all.

That leading man was Bob Geldof, lead singer for new wave band the Boomtown Rats, who'd had a substantial and controversial hit with "I Don't Like Mondays," in 1979. Geldof would later be knighted, in 1986, for his participation in humanitarian music projects like Band Aid, which recorded the benefit single "Do They Know It's Christmas" and spawned the Live Aid concert in the hopes of alleviating famine in Ethiopia. But circa 1981–82, the punky young rocker gave scant indication that he would one day become "Sir Bob." Though Geldof, like Waters, had had no prior acting experience, he brought a youthful energy and charisma to his portrayal of Pink, which helped associate *The Wall* with the new wave Eighties rather than the dinosaur Seventies. Waters' current feelings about having been eclipsed by Geldof are not known. Although on the voice-over commentary track that can be accessed on the DVD release of *The Wall* Waters can be heard poking fun at Geldof in a thick Irish brogue (Geldof is Irish) during one scene. It is one of several *Mystery Science Theater* moments that make the commentary the most hilarious aspect of the DVD, although perhaps inadvertently so.

Taking up the latter half of 1981 and the first half of '82, work on the film was fraught with tensions, just as the album sessions had been; and Waters ultimately clashed with Alan Parker. Waters had been persuaded to take a long-overdue vacation during the time period when much of the filming was completed. "But I hung around the editing suite quite a lot," he says, "much to the dismay of Alan Parker. That's sort of when our big fights really started."

The film was nonetheless completed and made its world premiere on July 14, 1982. It did well at the box office and later became a top-selling videocassette, enabling the band to more than recoup the money they'd lost on the concerts. *The Wall* movie has much of the naive narrative exuberance of the early MTV era. It's almost like a series of great video clips, ingeniously linked. High points include the grim, Dickensian assembly line of a school where "Another Brick in the Wall" is set, Gerald Scarfe's scary animation piece for "Goodbye Blue Sky" and "In the Flesh's" fascist rally sequence, which was staged using real English skinheads, who lend a chilling note of authenticity to the scenes.

Twenty years after the release of the original album, *The Wall* now stands at about midpoint in the rock era, roughly equidistant from Elvis Presley and Kid Rock. It occupies a pivotal place in rock history, a link between the epic grandeur of late Sixties rock and the anger of the post-grunge epoch.

Don't Leave Me Now

Roger Waters' working relationship with David Gilmour and Nick Mason lasted through one more album after *The Wall*: 1983's *The Final Cut*. Not long after the making of that record—a difficult process by most accounts—Waters parted company with his two former colleagues on somewhat less than friendly terms. Waters later lost a legal battle in which he sought to prevent Gilmour,

Mason and Wright from recording or performing under the name Pink Floyd. Waters' post-Floyd solo albums, *The Pros and Cons of Hitch Hiking* (1984), *Radio K.A.O.S.* (1987) and *Amused to Death* (1993) have been well received but have not had the same widespread pop culture impact of big Pink Floyd albums like *Dark Side of the Moon*, *Wish You Were Here* and *The Wall*.

It would seem that Waters' relationship with *The Wall* is an ongoing one, much like Pete Townshend's with *Tommy*. In 1990, Waters staged a mammoth charity performance of *The Wall* at the site of the Berlin Wall in Germany. Sinead O'Connor, Bryan Adams, Joni Mitchell, Van Morrison and the Band were among the star-studded cast, and the show was subsequently released on CD and video. The falling of the Berlin Wall seemed to bring a new poignancy to the central metaphor of Waters' piece. Like many fans of the work, Waters himself continues to find new meanings in *The Wall*. He is currently working on a theater adaptation.

"I'm trying to write some laughs into *The Wall*," he says. "You know there weren't very many. Maybe none at all. It's been problematic. Twenty years after having written the thing in the first place—and making the record and the movie and all that crap—I'm still not sure I understand the ending. But I've got a hell of a lot more ideas now then I did in 1979: what happens when you tear down the wall, and what's out there. I had no fucking idea back then. But maybe what I've discovered is that the answer to the question 'Is there anybody out there?' is ultimately no. That's not what's important. What's 'out there' is a projection. What's important is what's inside you. Of course contact with other people is important. But fundamentally, it's what's going on inside that's most important."

POSTSCRIPT

In 1985 Roger Waters served official notice that he was no longer a member of Pink Floyd. This notification took the form of letters sent to EMI and CBS Records—a legal nicety that enabled Waters to change management and get on with his solo career. And for a while in the mid Eighties, it looked as if the other members of Pink Floyd would go their separate ways as well. Dave Gilmour threw himself into work on his second solo record, 1984's *About Face*, enlisting the aid of his rock star pals Pete Townshend and Steve Winwood. A high profile career as a session guitarist also began to open up for Gilmour, who performed on Townshend's *White City* album, not to mention discs by Paul McCartney, Bryan Ferry and others.

Richard Wright teamed up with Dave "De" Harris from the band Fashion to release an album under the name Zee before retreating to his homes and yacht in the Greek islands. Nick Mason started up an advertising jingle company with guitarist Richard Fenn (10cc, Mike Oldfield). The duo also released an album as Profiles.

But, with the possible exception of Mason's jingle house, none of these post-Floyd projects was a rousing success. And as early as 1986, Gilmour moved forward with plans to reconvene Pink Floyd—without Roger Waters. The post-Waters incarnation of Pink Floyd went on to release two studio albums, *A Momentary Lapse of Reason* (1987) and *The Division Bell* (1994). Unlike the albums of Floyd's mid-Seventies heyday, however, these more recent discs rely heavily on contributions from top-flight session players. With characteristic acrimony, Waters has dubbed his former bandmates' efforts "the Floyd fraud."

In the late Eighties and Nineties, Pink Floyd's live shows came to be more of a focal point for fan interest than the band's studio releases. They've taken on the importance that Grateful Dead concerts had for devoted followers of that band—an opportunity to relive a golden era of rock history, especially for those who weren't even born when the original discs came out. In keeping with Pink Floyd's reputation, shows have become increasingly elaborate multimedia spectacles—grander in scope than anyone back at the UFO club in 1966 ever would have thought possible.

The success of the shows has been a thorn in the side of Waters, who performs Pink Floyd material at his own solo concerts. His position is that, as author of many of the best-known Floyd compositions (even if only the lyrics in some cases), this is his privilege and prerogative. The most ludicrous episode in Waters' legal efforts to prevent his former bandmates from touring and recording as Pink Floyd was his claim to artistic ownership of the giant inflatable pig image that has become one of the most beloved Pink Floyd stage props in the years since *Animals.* In one ploy to subvert Waters' claim, the other three Floyds changed the gender of the band's porcine mascot by equipping it with a prominent male appendage.

A real ballsy move, one might say. And proof that not even Roger Waters can dampen the enduring popularity of Pink Floyd.

Guitar World, July 1988

Absolute Sound

If the world didn't clamor for his searing guitar lines, David Gilmour would just be another semi-reclusive Englishman with a house in the country and an interesting collection of Strats.

By Bill Milkowski

It's 2010. A joint Soviet-American space mission has successfully established a sprawling colony of settlers on the moon. The two dozen cosmonauts, astronauts, scientists and assorted astronomers have been living in peace and harmony for nearly a year. Their general consul, made up of an equal-numbered contingent of Yanks and Ruskies, has set up a series of laws by which all abide. And they have chosen a national anthem for their Lunaville home. By majority vote, they picked Pink Floyd's *Dark Side of the Moon*, a 20th-century classic that is still, amazingly, surfacing in the *Billboard* charts back on Earth, nearly 40 years after its initial release.

David Gilmour, guitarist extraordinaire and only surviving member of Pink Floyd, is in his mid-sixties and still an active recording artist. His latest release, *Brain Spurs and Other Cognitive Mishaps*, is riding high on the *Billboard* Next Age charts, and the hologram of his hit single, "I Put a Mind Probe on You," is selling particularly well in the Soviet Union. Yet, in spite of the widespread popularity and critical acclaim he's enjoyed over the past 15 years as a solo artist, Gilmour still fondly recalls his days with the Floyd. The ever-selling *Dark Side of the Moon* holds a particularly special place in his memory banks, though when asked to list his favorite project over the past 40 years of his career, the sexagenarian axeman says, "Well, you know...I really quite liked A *Momentary Lapse of Reason*. I think my playing was rather good on that one, actually."

I would tend to agree with ol' man Gilmour on that. Sure, he has played some memorable solos since he joined Pink Floyd on February 18, 1968—"Comfortably Numb" from 1979's *The Wall*, "Pigs" from 1977's *Animals*, "All Lovers Are Deranged" from his 1984 solo project, *About Face*, to name just a few. But on *A Momentary Lapse of Reason*, the first Floyd album where Gilmour is truly and forcefully in the driver's seat (freed as he is from the domineering influence of his old nemesis Roger Waters, who split the Floyd to pursue a solo career), the guy is absolutely killin' with that Strat.

Make that a Strat and a Steinberger. On the cut "Sorrow," the man who has for so long been associated with Fender Stratocasters plugs in one of Ned's headless wonders, lays on the TransTrem and the results are earth-shaking.

"That very nasty distortion you hear at the beginning of the song is basically the result of the Steinberger going through two little amps in the studio—a Fender Super Champ and a Gallien-Krueger. I use a Boss Heavy Metal distortion pedal and a Boss digital delay pedal which then goes into the Fender Super Champ. And that in combination with the internal distortion on the Gallien-Krueger was how I got that particular sound.

"Funny enough," he adds, "I wrote the lyrics for the song first. I sat at home one night...I was kind of hoping the music would come out of the air and the song would magically write itself. But it didn't. But I did write all the lyrics that night and the next day I went into the studio, plugged in the Steinberger and that was what came out. I had no particular plan. I had just gotten the Steinberger and hadn't really played it all that much at that point. But I rather liked the sound it makes naturally. And then the combination of bending up with the wang bar on whole chords while simultaneously fading in with a stereo volume pedal...*that's the sound.*"

A very nasty sound indeed, guaranteed to please connoisseurs of "sick" guitar.

Elsewhere on *A Momentary Lapse of Reason*, Gilmour plays his familiar red Strat with typical lyricism, cut with a definite blues bite. His clean, economical lines on the instrumental "Signs of Life" (recorded direct to the desk with no effects whatsoever) features some classic Delta blues licks at the tag. And his piercing single-note work during his stinging exchanges with saxman Tom Scott on "Terminal Frost" is right out of the Albert Collins school of toe-curling blues riffs.

Gilmour admits a great love of the blues, but says that the key to his playing is his melodic sense. "Yes, there's a lot of the blues in my playing. When I was young, I actually sat down and learned many of the classic blues solos by Eric Clapton and Jimi Hendrix as well as studying old Howlin' Wolf records. But I don't consciously delve into that area now. Blues lines as such are fairly specific. It's like, you've got a series of things that you can put together in different combinations but there aren't that many moves you can make. Instead, I try to approach things, given my limitations and strengths, from a more melodic standpoint and just work on it until it sounds…nice. I don't really have any plan in hand that helps me to deal with this. I try not to be too tied down by rules and regulations. So the blues influence may come out at times but I like to think that I come at it from a different angle."

Strengths?

"Oh, I'd say my sense of melody. My sense of going for the unusual at times."

Weaknesses?

"Well, I can't really play fast, per se. Not like so many players today. I don't have a very disciplined approach to practicing or anything, but I do tend to have a guitar around most of the day. But about once a year I have sort of an attack of a guilty conscience about my abilities, so then I'll sit and run through a couple of scales. But generally, I'm not too ambitious about that sort of thing. I just tend to strap on the guitar in the studio and do something crazy.

"Again, I don't have a very precise method of doing anything. I'm sorry…I feel like I'm being awfully vague about all this, but that's the way I am. I just play intuitively and work the same way in the studio. I don't have any magical effects or anything that helps me to get my particular sound. It's all very hard to explain. I just keep fiddling with the little knobs on different boxes until it sounds right to me. I like to approach every track and every solo I do with an open mind. I don't really have any kind of general philosophy of playing, I don't think. And to be honest with you, I can't really remember how I achieved certain sounds in the studio. I don't really approach anything with any great plan, except that I work on the sound until it sounds right to me...forgetting instantly afterward how on earth it was done."

Okay, thanks for the workshop, Dave.

In this day and age of neo-classical-metal-whatever, where young (and I mean *young*, like 18) guitar daredevils are racing up and down the neck at inhuman speeds, skipping across strings like Evel Knievel hurtling a row of school buses on his cycle, blazing through scales and arpeggios like sewing machines on automatic pilot, David Gilmour stands out as an anomaly. Call him a throwback, a dinosaur, a relic, if you will. But for my money, he could teach these young whippersnappers a thing or two about phrasing, about finesse and taste, about making a personal statement on the instrument, not through any magical gadgets but through one's own personal touch...bare fingers on strings.

"One thing about my guitar sounds," offers the humble Floydman of few words, "I think I could walk into any music shop anywhere and with a guitar off the rack, a couple of basic pedals and an amp I could sound just like me. There's no devices, customized or otherwise, that give me my sound. It comes off my fingers. It all comes down to personal taste, I guess. Like vibrato, for instance. I like a kind of refined version, which I do either with a finger or with a wang bar...sometimes both at the same time. But I must say that a lot of vibrato that's used today just doesn't appeal to me at all. It doesn't sound musical."

Being a rich, semi-reclusive Englishman with a country home and family, Gilmour doesn't spend much time making the scene in London, New York or L.A., hanging with the cats, keeping up with the latest trends in music, the newest innovations in technique. He admits, for instance, to never having heard Yngwie Malmsteen or any of the clones who spun off from that school of playing. But he admits, "I do like Eddie Van Halen's playing a lot. Of course, I can't do that at all. I don't have the fingers for it."

Other players he admires?

"Steve Lukather is great. I really love his playing. I love a lot of people's playing, but I mostly tend to like some of the old guys, you know? Eric Clapton, Jeff Beck, people like that. They're more to my taste."

His taste comes basically out of the blues while young turks like Yngwie and his ilk basically shun the blues in favor of classical scales. As far as Gilmour is concerned, you can keep your Paganini scales and flourishes. He prefers the simple boogie-woogie of John Lee Hooker and the dirty urban blues of Muddy Waters, which he pays tribute to on "Dogs of War," a sort of symphonic slow boogie blues with a whole section of sampled cellos droning that familiar ostinato riff. Simple, yes, but full of feeling, especially when Gilmour sails over the top with his slightly wet, as opposed to the standard dry, treble-piercing shrieks that many young guitar phenoms seem to prefer today.

Yeah, so David's a dinosaur. Fine. But I'll take his solo on "Yet Another Movie" over 90 percent of the flailing fretboard work on record today. Of all the tunes on *A Momentary Lapse of Reason*, this is perhaps his most thoughtful, well-crafted solo of the bunch. That, and his moving solo on the anthemic "On the Turning Away," based on a traditional Celtic melody. On both tunes he takes his time and builds the solos artfully. Rather than just a series of tricky licks, he seems to orchestrate his statements carefully for maximum emotional effect, and yet he doesn't work out these solos ahead of time. Gilmour's finest solos are like spontaneous compositions. There's tension and release, statements and resolutions. And like Carlos Santana and the whole lineage of bluesmen from T-Bone Walker to Otis Rush to Eric Clapton, he knows how to squeeze every bit of juice out of a single note. He savors each note before going on to the next, and he comes up for air (take that, speedmongers).

I sound like a curmudgeon. I'm sorry, that's the way I feel. That's the way David Gilmour feels, too. We're both dinosaurs in this day and age. But if the old adage What Goes Around Comes Around is actually true, Gilmour's music, that *sound*, will be around long after all the Yngwie clones have been put out to pasture. After all, whose music did the joint Soviet-American colony on the moon choose for their national anthem? I rest my case.

Any parting advice for young guitarists, Dave?

"Well, it's very hard to advise people, but in general I would say listen to as many different types of music as you can. And don't worry. Let everything come out of you in whatever way feels right, rather than wasting a lot of time and energy in trying to be someone else. That's what I'm trying to do myself."

And succeeding quite well, I might add.

Guitar World, February 1993

David's Harp

David Gilmour reflects on his creative partnership with Roger Waters and his own role in making Pink Floyd one of rock's most innovative and experimental bands.

By Alan di Perna

Amid the psychedelic explosion of new groups making their debut in the charmed world that was London, 1967, was a quartet called the Pink Floyd. In small, smoky clubs like UFO and the Roundhouse, the Floyd galvanized the London scene with their extended, free-form instrumental jams. Fledgling flower children grooved to the heady new sounds in rooms that seemed to bob and levitate as blobs of multicolored liquid light melted the walls around them. Perhaps even more than Cream and the Jimi Hendrix Experience, two other groups that debuted in '67, the Pink Floyd were psychedelia personified.

By the following year, however, the band was forced to confront the rapidly deteriorating mental condition of Syd Barrett, their brilliant but unstable guitarist and leader. In 1968 the Pink Floyd dropped the "The" from their name—and they dropped Syd Barrett. Guitarist David Gilmour, an old school friend of Syd's, was drafted to replace him. Unquestionably, Barrett invented the Pink Floyd, and his troubled genius would later furnish the subject matter for some of the band's best songs. But it was David Gilmour and his lyrical guitar work that provided Pink Floyd with the sonic signature that helped carry them to international stardom in the Seventies, when the smoky clubs of their swinging London days gave way to vast arenas and stadiums. The Floyd's ever-evolving trippy instrumental textures reached the highest levels of complexity, perfectly complementing their otherworldly concert visuals.

Pink Floyd's next big crack-up didn't occur until 1985, when David Gilmour and bassist Roger Waters came to a bitter parting of the ways. Gilmour assumed sole leadership of the band in 1987. With Waters' brooding lyrics out of the mix, Gilmour's searing, expansive guitar style—the core of the band's sound since its Flower Power days—assumed an even greater importance.

These days, David Gilmour is a distinguished, gray-haired English gentleman who becomes instantly youthful once he gets a guitar in his hands. In celebration of *Shine On* (Columbia), the new Pink Floyd box set, Gilmour consented to share some of his memories with *Guitar World*.

GUITAR WORLD Long before Pink Floyd, you and Syd Barrett hung out together in college, in Cambridge, playing guitars. Can you recall what you played or how you influenced each other?

DAVID GILMOUR We were friends first, then we picked up guitars later on. I was playing professionally in groups before Syd. So, technically speaking, I was a little better than Syd when we were at college. We sat around learning Beatles songs, Rolling Stones songs, r&b, blues songs...I can recall spending some time working on "Come On," the first Stones B side or whatever it was, working all that out, playing harmonicas and stuff. He'd know something, I'd know something and we'd just swap, as people do in back rooms everywhere. He then left that college and moved up to an art college in London, which is when Pink Floyd got formed.

GW There's a famous story about Syd being phased out of the band in 1968. You were all in a van, on your way to a gig in Southampton...

GILMOUR Not in a van, no. In a Bentley.

GW Right. And someone said, "Oh, let's just not pick up Syd tonight." Can you recall who said that?

GILMOUR Probably Roger. Certainly not me—I was the new boy. I was in the back. Someone probably said, "Shall we go and pick up Syd?" And Roger probably said [*in conspiratorial tones*], "Oh no, let's not!" And off we went down to Southampton. We were playing with the Incredible String Band and Tyrannosaurus Rex that night.

GW In the early days of Pink Floyd, did you feel like you were just a Syd surrogate?

GILMOUR Oh, I was; no question about it. They wanted me to play his parts and sing his songs. Nobody else wanted to sing them, and I got elected. That was my job as far as live shows were concerned, anyway. Me and Syd played only five gigs together in Pink Floyd. Or maybe four. Maybe Southampton was supposed to be the fifth one; I don't remember. While all this was happening, we were also trying to make the new album, *A Saucerful of Secrets*. But live, we didn't play the tracks from that, but virtually all Syd's stuff. Because there wasn't anything else to do. It was either that or back to Bo Diddley covers.

"A SAUCERFUL OF SECRETS"

A Saucerful of Secrets (1968)

GW What made the band decide to take on a lengthy, abstract instrumental like "Saucerful"?

GILMOUR That's hard to say. I had just joined the group shortly before that. I don't think the band really knew quite where they wanted to go after Syd's departure. "A Saucerful of Secrets" was a very important track; it gave us our direction forward. If you take "A Saucerful of Secrets," "Atom Heart Mother" [Atom Heart Mother, *1970*] and "Echoes" [Meddle, *1971*], all lead logically to *Dark Side of the Moon*. "A Saucerful" was inspired when Roger and Nick [*Mason, Pink Floyd's drummer*] began drawing weird shapes on a piece of paper. We then composed music based on the structure of the drawing.

GW You mean you used the drawing to diagram the dynamics?

GILMOUR Yeah. We tried to write the music around the peaks and valleys of the art. My role, I suppose, was to try and make it a bit more musical, and to help create a balance between formlessness and structure, disharmony and harmony.

GW There are varying opinions as to whether or not Syd is on the "Saucerful of Secrets" track.

GILMOUR No, he's not. That's totally false. He's on three or four other tracks on the album, including "Remember a Day" and "Jugband Blues" [*Syd's sole composition on the* Saucerful *album*]. He's also on a tiny bit of "Set the Controls for the Heart of the Sun." I think I'm on "Set the Controls" as well.

GW Can you recall any of the techniques you used to get unusual guitar tones back then?

GILMOUR Well, on the middle section of "A Saucerful of Secrets," most of the time the guitar was lying on the studio floor. You know how mic stands have three steel legs about a foot long? I unscrewed one of the legs and just whizzed one of those up and down the neck—not very subtly. Another technique, which came a bit later, involved taking a small piece of steel and rubbing it from side to side across the strings. You just move it and stop it in places that sound good. It's something like an EBow.

"ONE OF THESE DAYS"

Meddle (1971)

GW Another technical point: the instrumental "One of These Days" was born when someone plugged a bass into a "Binson Echorec." What is this device?

GILMOUR The Binson was an Italian-made delay unit. It was strange because it didn't utilize tape loops, but used a metal recording wheel instead. [*Binson's Echorec was basically a wire recorder—a precursor to magnetic tape. It had six knobs, an input volume, one to control the length, volume and tone of a swell, a three-position selector knob and a 12-position switching knob. The selector accessed either echo (one repeat), repeat (more than one repeat) or swell (reverbs cleverly devised by feeding the outputs of the heads back to themselves), while the switching knob accessed 12 variations of these.*] You could get some wonderful delay effects that aren't attainable on anything that's been made since. "One of These Days" evolved from some of my experiments with the Binson, as did "Echoes" [*also from* Meddle]. One day, Roger decided to take some of the techniques that I was developing and try them out for himself on bass. And he came up with that basic riff that we all worked on and turned into "One of These Days." For the middle section, another piece of technology came into play: an

H&H amp with vibrato. I set the vibrato to more or less the same tempo as the delay. But the delay was in 3/4 increments of the beat while the vibrato went with the beat. I just played the bass through it and made up that little section, which we then stuck on to a bit of tape and edited in. The tape splices were then camouflaged with cymbal crashes.

GW So you played the bass on that track?

GILMOUR Yes. The opening section is me and Roger. On "One of These Days," for some reason, we decided to do a double track of the bass. You can actually hear it if you listen in stereo. The first bass is me. A bar later, Roger joins in on the other side of the stereo picture. We didn't have a spare set of strings for the spare bass guitar, so the second bass is very dull-sounding. [*laughs*] We sent a roadie out to buy some strings, but he wandered off to see his girlfriend instead.

GW How did you hit on the idea of playing slide guitar on the track?

GILMOUR I guess I was never particularly confident in my ability as a pure guitar player, so I would try any trick in the book. I'd always liked lap steels, pedal steels and things like that. I can't remember exactly what I used on "One of These Days"; I may have bought a lap steel by that point, but maybe I used a regular guitar. When I tour, I use two cheap Jensen lap steels customized with Fender pickups for slide parts. The lap steel on "One of These Days" is tuned to an open E minor chord—E B E G B E low to high. The other lap steel is basically tuned to a modified open G chord [*D G D G B E, low to high*]. I use that for "The Great Gig in the Sky." You'll notice that I kept the top string tuned to an E so that I could do major and minor chords on the first three strings.

The one thing I don't do is regular slide guitar with the thingie on your finger. I've never had any interest in that.

"MONEY"

Dark Side of the Moon (1973)

GW Where did the famous 7/4 time signature for "Money" originate?

GILMOUR It's Roger's riff. Roger came in with the verses and lyrics to "Money" more or less completed. And we just made up middle sections, guitar solos and all that stuff. We also invented some new riffs—we created a 4/4 progression for the guitar solo and made the poor saxophone player play in 7/4. It was my idea to break down and become dry and empty for the second chorus of the solo.

GW Were you purposely trying to get away from just playing a 12-bar blues on guitar?

GILMOUR No, I just wanted to make a dramatic effect with the three solos. The first solo is ADT'd—Artificially Double-Tracked. And the third one is actually double-tracked. I think I did the first two solos on a Fender Stratocaster, but the last one was done on a different guitar—a Lewis, which was made by some guy in Vancouver. It had a whole two octaves on the neck, which meant I could get up to notes that I couldn't play on a Stratocaster.

David Gilmour (left) and Nick Mason (right), live in 1973.

Michael Putland/Retna

GW What amp did you use on that?

GILMOUR I imagine it was a Hiwatt, but I'm not too certain. I used Fender Twin Reverbs in the studio a lot, too. But I'm certain the effects consisted of a Fuzzface fuzz box and the Binson echo/delay.

GW What was [*producer/engineer*] Chris Thomas' role on *Dark Side of the Moon*?

GILMOUR Chris Thomas came in for the mixes, and his role was essentially to stop the arguments between me and Roger about how it should be mixed. I wanted *Dark Side* to be big and swampy and wet, with reverbs and things like that. And Roger was very keen on it being a very dry album. I think he was influenced a lot by John Lennon's first solo album [Plastic Ono Band], which was very dry. We argued so much that it was suggested we get a third opinion. We were going to leave Chris to mix it on his own, with Alan Parsons engineering. And of course on the first day I found out that Roger sneaked in there. So the second day I sneaked in there. And from then on, we both sat right at Chris' shoulder, interfering. Luckily, Chris was more sympathetic to my point of view than he was to Roger's.

GW Was that the first album where tension emerged between you and Roger?

GILMOUR Ah, there's always been tension. But it was all quite controllable until after the *Wall* album.

GW There's creative tension and then there's outright hostility...

GILMOUR There's creative tension and there's total egocentric megalomaniacal tension, if you like.

GW Did the prospect of having to follow the huge success of *Dark Side of the Moon* create a lot of pressure on you during the sessions for *Wish You Were Here*?

GILMOUR Yeah, that's what the album's about, I think as far as Roger's concerned anyway. It's about that feeling we were left with at the end of *Dark Side*—that feeling of "What do you do when you've done everything?" But I think we got over that. And for me, *Wish You Were Here* is the most satisfying album. I really love it. I mean, I'd rather listen to that than *Dark Side of the Moon*. Because I think we achieved a better balance of music and lyrics on *Wish You*

Were Here. Dark Side went a bit too far the other way—too much into the importance of the lyrics. And sometimes the tunes—the vehicles for the lyrics—got neglected. To me, one of Roger's failings is that sometimes, in his effort to get the words across, he uses a less-than-perfect vehicle.

"DOGS"

Animals (1977)

GW On the next Pink Floyd album, *Animals*, "Dogs" is the only song not written solely by Roger. What was your part in co-writing "Dogs" with him?

GILMOUR I basically wrote all the chords—the main music part of it. And we wrote some other bits together at the end.

GW What did you play on that?

GILMOUR A custom Telecaster. I was coming through some Hiwatt amps and a couple of Yamaha rotating speaker cabinets—Leslie-style cabinets that they used to make. I used to use two of those onstage along with the regular amps. That slight Leslie effect made a big difference in the sound.

GW Throughout the Seventies and Eighties, each successive Pink Floyd album grew slightly more elaborate. Was it difficult to reflect that growth on stage?

GILMOUR Actually, very difficult. We spent years gathering experts around us—just gaining the necessary expertise in all the areas we wanted to be good in. It was always a lot of work, but we looked forward to playing.

GW Would you say you felt more at ease in the very early days of the band's free-form psychedelic experimentation onstage, or in the later period, when you relied more on carefully orchestrated stage extravaganzas?

GILMOUR Somewhere in the middle, really. For me, the *Wall* show was terrific fun, and a great achievement. But I had to take on the role of music director, if you like, and deal with a lot of purely mechanical things onstage so that Roger didn't have to think about them. I had a huge cue sheet up on my amps, because we had all these cues coming up on monitors or on screen and different delay settings which I had to transmit with very primitive equipment to all the delay lines onstage. Very tricky. Once you got over being satisfied with how clever it was and how wonderfully it all worked, there were virtually no moments except for the solo in "Comfortably Numb" when you could say, "Forget it, just blow. Just play." Having said all that, though, I should add that I like structure. I'm very keen on melody, I'm a big Beatles fan, and just about everything else I love—like the blues—is highly structured. Totally free-forming is not my thing. But totally rigid structure isn't either.

"COMFORTABLY NUMB"

The Wall (1979)

GW "Comfortably Numb" is one of your few co-writing credits on *The Wall*. By all reports, it wasn't born easily.

GILMOUR Well, there were two recordings of that which me and Roger argued about. I'd written it when I was doing my first solo album [David Gilmour, *1978*]. We changed the key of the song's opening from E to B, I think. The verse stayed exactly the same. Then we had to add a little bit because Roger wanted to do the line, "I have become comfortably numb." Other than that, it was very, very simple to write. But the arguments were over how it should be mixed and which track we should use. We'd done one track with Nick Mason on drums that I thought was too rough and sloppy. We had another go at it, and I thought that the second take was better. Roger disagreed. It was more an ego thing than anything else. We really went head to head with each other over such a minor thing.

GW Have disagreements between you and Roger ever reached the point of physical violence?

GILMOUR They've threatened to. But it's never actually come to that. Once Roger and I had a real shouting match at this Italian restaurant in North Hollywood. We'd gone there with [*producer*] Bob Ezrin to have it out over something on *The Wall*—probably "Comfortably Numb," because the only thing I'd really argue with Roger over was my own music. With his music, I wouldn't bother to argue.

GW While the earlier Pink Floyd records were concept albums, *The Wall* is the first one with an outright plot. What were your feelings about that?

GILMOUR I *liked* Roger's story line. Although I didn't totally agree with it, you've got to let a chap have his vision. I just had a different view of our relationship with our audience than Roger did. Roger didn't like touring. And he felt there was no connection between him and the audience that were in front of him. I had a different view of it; I still do. And my view of what *The Wall* itself is about is more jaundiced today than it was then. It appears now to be a catalog of people Roger blames for his own failings in life, a list of "you fucked me up this way, you fucked me up that way."

GW What about your solo on "Comfortably Numb"? Did that take a long time to develop?

GILMOUR No. I just went out into the studio and banged out five or six solos. From there I just followed my usual procedure, which is to listen back to each solo and mark out bar lines, noting which bits are good. In other words, I make a chart, putting ticks and crosses on different bars as I count through—two ticks if it's really good, one if it's good, and a cross if it's no go. Then I just follow the chart, whipping one fader up, then another fader, jumping from phrase to phrase and trying to make a really nice solo all the way through. That's the way we did it on "Comfortably Numb." It wasn't that difficult. But sometimes you find yourself jumping from one note to another in an impossible way. Then you have to go to another place and find a transition that sounds more natural.

GW When you do a comp like that, are you concerned that you'll wind up with a result that's physically impossible to play?

GILMOUR Not if it sounds all right. I'm perfectly happy to puzzle the hell out of people who try to work out how it was done.

GW You've got an extensive guitar collection—a world-famous collection. When you go to record, how much of it goes into the studio with you?

GILMOUR Well…not much, really. Generally, I just use a Stratocaster and that's the end of it. The ones I tend to use these days are modern '57 reissue Strats with EMG pickups. Apart from that, I've got a few different acoustics and slide guitars. For some of the rhythm things, I have a black Gretsch Duo-Sonic that sounds really nice.

GW Who are your favorite guitar players?

GILMOUR I'm not a fan of many rock guitar players. Jeff Beck's my favorite; a damned fine player.

GW You're not keen on the modern technical schools of guitar?

GILMOUR No. It's probably just sour grapes, because I'll never be able to do it. Eddie Van Halen has done a few things that I like a lot. But for the most part, no, that kind of thing doesn't interest me. Guitar just happens to be the instrument I can best express my feelings on. I'm not very fast on it, but you don't have to be. You hear something like John Lee Hooker doing "Dimples." Between the vocal lines he just hits the bottom string on the guitar—boom!—that one note says it all. My guitar influences are people like Pete Seeger, Leadbelly, Hank Marvin and Jeff Beck. But there hasn't been anyone recently that I've been turned on by.

GW It's great to hear you acknowledge a guy like Pete Seeger.

GILMOUR Oh, Pete Seeger's a wonderful, fantastic human being. "America's Tuning Fork," they called him at one time. I learned guitar off his *Pete Seeger Teaches Guitar* record. That was the first instruction I had. The first track taught you how to tune the guitar. That was pretty important.

"ONE SLIP"

A Momentary Lapse of Reason (1987)

GW Let's move on to Pink Floyd's most recent studio album, A *Momentary Lapse of Reason*. How did you hook up with Roxy Music's Phil Manzanera to write "One Slip"?

GILMOUR Phil is an old friend of mine. We've known each other for years and years, and we always talked about doing something together. So I went and visited him over at his studio, and we started playing around. During that whole period of time, I was trying things out with a number of people, to see if there was anyone I felt comfortable working with who could help to make the load a little lighter in doing the new Pink Floyd record without Roger. Phil basically wrote the music to "One Slip."

GW On *A Momentary Lapse*, how did you deal with the whole issue of maintaining continuity with the old Pink Floyd?

GILMOUR By totally ignoring it. I didn't bother with any of that stuff. I know it's something that came up in Bob Ezrin's mind; he felt a certain responsibility to make it sound like Pink Floyd. But that's something I had no interest in whatsoever. If it's done by me, it's going to sound like Pink Floyd to a certain extent. Because it's my voice, my guitar playing and my musical taste that are plastered all over everything Pink Floyd ever did, going back to *A Saucerful of Secrets*.

GW *A Momentary Lapse* is certainly a return to the lushness of pre-*Animals* Pink Floyd.

GILMOUR Yes. That's what I like. "Signs of Life," for example, is actually an old demo. I had to re-record a lot of things, but the rhythm guitar chords in the background are from a demo from way back in '78.

GW So on *A Momentary Lapse* you got to follow through on ideas that, perhaps because of Roger's dominance, you didn't get to pursue earlier?

GILMOUR Yeah. I went back to this balance of more music and not quite the same preponderance of words. You do what you're good at, you see. Roger's very good at lyrics. I'm certainly not as practiced as him, so I wouldn't put myself up there.

GW Was *A Momentary Lapse* a good experience for you, Nick and Rick [*Wright, Pink Floyd keyboardist*] in the sense that you assured yourselves that you could do it without Roger?

GILMOUR Yes. The album and the tour were a rehabilitative process for all of us.

GW It was good to hear you and Rick playing together again. [*Wright, ejected from the band in 1979, rejoined for* A Momentary Lapse.] The guitar and keyboards worked together so sympathetically on a lot of these old tracks we've been talking about.

GILMOUR Well, it's like Bob Dylan says [*in "My Back Pages"*]: "I was so much older then, I'm younger than that now." You learn things about yourself and other people as time goes by. When the three of us sit down and play, it sounds like Pink Floyd. There's a very distinct value in that which was important for me to discover. There's something there that's bigger than any one person's ego.

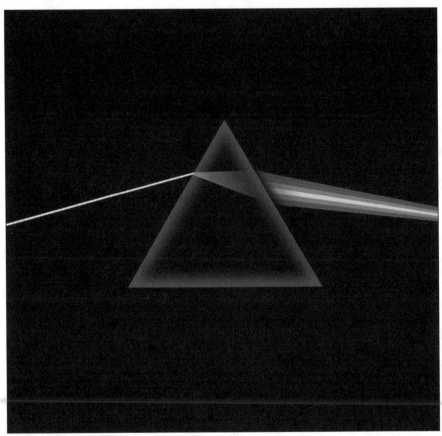

Album Cover of 1973's *Dark Side of the Moon*.

Guitar World, February 1993

Wall of Sound

The *Wall* producer Bob Ezrin and *Dark Side of the Moon* engineer Alan Parsons reveal a saucerful of studio secrets.

By Alan di Perna & Brad Tolinski

BOB EZRIN

How do you reason with two guys who once went to court over the artistic ownership of a big rubber pig? That was Bob Ezrin's mission when, during sessions for *The Wall* in 1979, he agreed to co-produce the album with David Gilmour and Roger Waters. At the time, the legendary tensions between the two feuding Floyds had come to a head.

"My job was to be Henry Kissinger—to mediate between two dominant personalities," recalls Ezrin from the safe perspective of 12 years. "Each one has a need to express himself in his own style. And sometimes those styles are very different."

Seasoned by sessions with Lou Reed, Alice Cooper and Kiss, Ezrin was the ideal man to co-produce *The Wall*. He first discussed the project with Roger Waters "during the *Animals* tour, in the back of Waters' limousine on the way to Hamilton, Ontario," recalls Ezrin. "He told me that because he felt so alienated, he had this concept of building a wall between the band and the audience. We kicked the idea around in the car. Honestly, I never expected anything to come of it."

But soon Ezrin found himself in the thick of Pink Floyd's most ambitious recording up to that time. No mere referee, he had plenty of his own ideas for *The Wall*: "I fought for the introduction of the orchestra on that record—the expansion of the Floyd's sound to something that was more orchestral, theatrical…'filmic' is the word. This became a big issue on 'Comfortably Numb,' which Dave saw as a more bare-bones track, with just bass, drums and guitar. Roger sided with me. So 'Comfortably Numb' is a true collaboration—it's David's music, Roger's lyric and my orchestral chart."

David Gilmour's classic guitar solo on "Comfortably Numb," says Ezrin, was cut using a combination of the guitarist's Hiwatt amps and Yamaha rotating speaker cabinets. But with Gilmour, he adds, equipment is secondary to touch: "You can give him a ukulele and he'll make it sound like a Stradivarius. He's truly got the best set of hands with which I've ever worked. People always ask me, 'How the hell did you get that astounding guitar sound at the end of "Another Brick in the Wall"?' That's just Dave direct, with a little compression. We used a form of double compression: first we put the guitar through a very aggressive limiting amplifier, compressed that output and overdrove it. The limiting amplifier makes it pop, and the compressor gives it a kind of density: the sound of being right in your face. But still, it's nothing so involved that it would have made that part sound good if Dave's playing hadn't been so brilliant. That's his first take, too!"

Ezrin was also called in to assist at the birth of the first (and, so far, the only) Pink Floyd studio album without Roger Waters: 1987's *A Momentary Lapse of Reason*. Here a different kind of artistic debate arose. While Gilmour was keen to strike out in new musical directions, Ezrin felt a certain obligation to produce a record that wouldn't disappoint the expectations of longtime Floyd fans.

"People are used to Pink Floyd delivering atmospheric, philosophical records, with lots of effects and ear candy," says Ezrin. "I didn't feel that a complete overhaul of the Pink Floyd sound or approach was called for at that time, particularly since Roger had left."

Given the disparate set of songs that had been written for the album, Ezrin and Gilmour keenly felt the need to find a common thread to hold them together. They found that thread in a most unexpected place: right under their feet. Ezrin and Gilmour were recording on the guitarist's studio boat, the Astoria, moored at the time on the River Thames. "Working on that boat was the most magical recording experience I've ever had," says Ezrin. "Sitting every day and watching the geese fly, the school-kids rowing, and the little old English fishermen on the bank created a kind of river atmosphere that permeates the whole album."

On a more practical level, the floating studio posed a few problems when it came to engineering guitar sounds. "It's not a huge environment," explains Ezrin. "So we couldn't keep the amps in the same room with us, and we were forced to use slightly smaller ones. But after playing around with them in the demo stages of the project, we found that we really liked that sound. So a Fender Princeton and a little G&K amp became the backbone of Dave's guitar sound for that record."

When the song "A New Machine" created the need for something slightly larger, Ezrin and Gilmour responded on a grand scale. "We actually hired a 24-track truck and a huge P.A. system and brought them inside the L.A. Sports Arena," the producer recalls. "We had the whole venue to ourselves, and we piped Dave's guitar tracks out into the arena and re-recorded them in 3D. So the tracks that originally came from a teeny little Gallien-Krueger and a teeny little Fender were piped through this enormous P.A. out into a sports arena, creating a sound like the Guitar from Hell."

But what of the fabled big rubber pig? Well, Roger Waters claimed copyright ownership of the oversized prop, used at countless Pink Floyd live shows. But David Gilmour had a huge male appendage fashioned for the creature—thereby altering "its" artistic character enough to get around the copyright. Gilmour defiantly flaunted the porcine symbol during the Floyd's Waters-less tour for *A Momentary Lapse of Reason*.

Aren't you glad you never had to settle studio arguments between these two?

—A. di P.

ALAN PARSONS

"Working with Pink Floyd is an engineer's dream, so I tried to take advantage of the situation," says studio wizard Alan Parsons with a touch of modesty. "*Dark Side of the Moon* came at a crucial stage in my career, so I was highly motivated. It was important to me, and I wanted to be sure that the job was done right."

Parsons' attention to detail obviously paid off: He won a Grammy Award for the best-engineered album of 1973, and *Dark Side of the Moon* went on to ride the charts for a record-breaking 14 years. More than just an engineer, Parsons also functioned as Pink Floyd's chief sonic architect. In addition to capturing the band's inspired performances on tape and crafting *Dark Side*'s celebrated three-dimensional mix, Parsons was also responsible for creating the album's twisted array of heartbeats, footsteps, clocks, airplanes and cash registers.

Understandably, Parsons asserts that it's "difficult to remember all the details of something that happened 20 years ago." Nonetheless, he gamely tried to field all questions related to one of rock's great milestones.

GUITAR WORLD How did you become Pink Floyd's engineer?

ALAN PARSONS It was simply through my staff position at Abbey Road Studios. I mixed Floyd's *Atom Heart Mother* and they liked my work, so they recruited me to work on the sessions for *Dark Side of the Moon*.

GW Did *Dark Side*'s three-dimensional sound evolve over a period of time, or was it planned from the beginning of the project?

PARSONS Nothing specific was said, but Pink Floyd had a reputation for creating records that were in a class of their own. They obviously wanted something special.

GW Do you have any particularly vivid memories of those sessions?

PARSONS There are a couple. I have some fond memories of being left alone every once in a while to do rough mixes. Those were in the days when the comedy group Monty Python was popular, and the band would often leave the studio to watch them on television. I would stay behind and work, and it was during those times that I would get my best ideas. One of my contributions was to add the footsteps to the "On the Run" sequence. There were no band members present—it was just me with my assistant engineer, Peter James. Poor Peter had the job of running back and forth while I recorded him.

I remember instructing him to do things like "breathe harder." [*laughs*] I was also responsible for the clocks in "Time," which I'd originally recorded at an antiques store for a sound-effects record. Each clock was recorded separately, and we just blended them together.

GW Did the band compose much of the album's material in the studio?

PARSONS Not really. They'd already performed a version of *Dark Side* in concert before they went into the studio. It was originally called *Eclipse*.

GW What about "On the Run"? I always assumed that it was created in the studio.

PARSONS You're right. "On the Run" is an exception. That was pretty much Dave's studio creation. He programmed a random sequence into an early VCS3 synthesizer and experimented until he found something he liked. All the basic sounds—including the bass and percussion sounds—came as a mono feed from that one synth. It's funny, because most people assume that "On the Run" is composed of several overdubs. It's actually a one-off performance.

GW Were there any specific technological factors that contributed to the album's space-age sound?

PARSONS *Dark Side* was recorded at a time when quadraphonic systems [*systems using four channels to record and reproduce sound*] appeared to be on the horizon. For example, a lot of the effects on the album were designed with quad reproduction in mind—most notably the introduction to "Money." The idea was that each part of the cash register would emanate from a different speaker. As a result, lots of time was spent recording each segment of the sound effect on discrete channels. Obviously, no one knew that quad systems would eventually fizzle, but I would say that thinking in quadraphonic terms probably made us more careful about how we recorded the effects.

GW David Gilmour's guitar sound on *Dark Side* is massive. Do you recall how it was recorded?

PARSONS David was very much in control of his sound system. We rarely added effects to his guitar in the control room. Generally speaking, the sound on the album is pretty much what came out of his amp. As I recall, he used a Hiwatt stack and a Binson Echorec for delays.

GW What kind of board did you use?

PARSONS A custom-built, late-generation 16-track EMI board. It's been reported that we used a 24-track board, but that's not true. Believe it or not, almost all the tracks are second generation. We often ran out of tracks and had to bounce.

GW Do you think *Dark Side* could have been recorded using today's colder-sounding digital equipment?

PARSONS I don't see why not. The album is just the combination of four talented people with some good songs and good ideas. These days, the only difference is that it's difficult to be original with sound. Those Japanese black boxes just make it too easy to dial up good sounds, but not necessarily original ones. Back then, we really had to work at it. It was literally a fight to reset the delay effect on "Us and Them." We spent a tremendous amount of time hooking up Dolby units and realigning machines at the wrong tape speed to accomplish that effect. "Us and Them" was all done with tape delays because digital delays didn't exist then. All these things took hours to set up.

GW I understand that you helped remaster the CD edition of *Dark Side of the Moon* for the *Shine On* Pink Floyd box set.

PARSONS That is correct. I received a call from James Guthrie, who became the band's engineer after I left. He was supervising the remastering of the Pink Floyd box, and he needed some technical information regarding those sessions. I happened to be in the vicinity of the studio where he was remastering, so I went down.

Basically, we discovered that the master tapes were in pretty good shape, and all we had to do was add a little brightness to the top end of the tracks. I felt very pleased with what we did, and feel that the version of *DSOTM* on *Shine On* is the definitive version.

—B.T.

Album cover of 1994's *The Division Bell.*

Guitar World, September 1994

Sounds of Silence

In this exclusive interview, the ordinarily reserved David Gilmour discusses his perspective—personal, political and musical—on Pink Floyd's brilliant 1994 album, *The Division Bell.*

By Brad Tolinski

With a No. 1 album, a high-profile stadium tour and non-stop radio airplay, Pink Floyd appear to be everywhere—and, oddly, nowhere.

In an era when MTV appearances and revealing magazine interviews are de rigueur for rock stars on the make, the members of Floyd have methodically kept the media at bay. You won't find their mugs plastered on the cover of *Rolling Stone* or *Entertainment Weekly*. Don't expect to see them on Letterman anytime soon. In fact, if you happen to be lucky enough to scalp a ticket to one of their sold-out shows, you may even miss them on-stage. Shrouded by state-of-the-art stage production, the band performs their spacey anthems while obscured by clouds of dry ice and laser technology.

And group leader David Gilmour wouldn't have it any other way.

Sporting a fresh crew cut and dressed in meticulously pressed black clothes, the earnest guitarist/vocalist could easily pass for one of the hipper, graying, urban professionals that comprise part of his audience.

"I cannot tell you how happy I am about the accidents and the choices that have brought me to the place where I can sing what I want to, get paid very well for it and still be able to live like a normal human being," Gilmour says with visible relief. "It's having the best of all possible worlds.

"Occasionally I get these sort of out-of-body experiences when I'm onstage, standing in front of maybe 60,000 people. I look at myself, thinking, Good Lord, how on earth did this happen? One part of my brain is fully focused on performing and the other part is somewhere else, thinking, How extraordinary it is—but how lucky I am!"

Lucky, yes; happy—that's another story. Pink Floyd's brilliant new recording, *The Division Bell* (Columbia), strongly suggests that Gilmour still has one or two personal demons rattling around his cage. The album—named after the bell in the British House of Commons that summons members to parliamentary debate—is a thinly veiled documentary of the guitarist's battle-scarred relationships with the women in his life and with ex-bandmate Roger Waters. Considering the recording's delicate subject matter, it's little wonder that he exercises his right to be selective about who he talks to.

MONTREAL, CANADA—A crew numbering well over 100 scurry around making last-minute preparations for the second of three sold-out Pink Floyd concerts at the city's Olympia Stadium. The 180-foot stage, constructed from 700 tons of steel with its 130-foot arch, is truly miraculous, an appropriate launching pad for one of the most visually ambitious tours in rock history. Soon, it will spring to life and dazzle over 80,000 Floyd fanatics with a light show designed to make the aurora borealis look like a dime store sparkler. Gilmour promises to chat after a quick afternoon rehearsal with Floyd's expanded road band, which features keyboardist Rick Wright and drummer Nick Mason, both original members, as well as seven additional musicians. The rehearsal begins with Gilmour leading the group through a powerful version of "Eclipse," the majestic grand finale to the haunting best-seller *Dark Side of the Moon*. The band plays it through three more times, effecting minor changes in tempo and dynamics with each performance.

Suddenly, in a fleeting moment between takes, the ensemble, with the exception of Gilmour, launches into a raucous version of Led Zeppelin's "Whole Lotta Love." Floyd playing Zep—truly a classic Classic Rock moment! But it immediately becomes apparent that taskmaster Gilmour is not amused. "Love" quickly peters out, and it's back to the business at hand. The rehearsal finishes 30 minutes later, and David is ready to speak. When asked about the band's impromptu Zeppelin jam, the soft-spoken Englishman deadpans, "Oh yes, I docked them a week's wages for that."

Gilmour is extremely polite throughout our encounter, but he never lets his guard down. Secrecy has always been an essential component of the Pink Floyd mystique, and he dispenses information sparingly. "I don't like to get too specific about lyrics," he warns. "It places limitations on them, and spoils the listener's interpretation." He is similarly reluctant to talk about his instrument, explaining that he gets "really bored of talking about guitars and amps because I just can't remember what I used on anything."

But as the conversation progresses, the reticent rocker opens up—and the walls come tumbling down.

GUITAR WORLD Why have you been so reluctant to discuss *The Division Bell*?

DAVID GILMOUR I found that there's very little that one wants to say about it. I mean, I don't know if it's just a stage in my life, but I just don't feel like saying very much about how I write songs and what they mean and all that sort of stuff. But we'll give it a whirl. I'm not trying to be unhelpful. Forgive me. It's got nothing to do with anything except me.

GW Fair enough. Overall, *The Division Bell* seems to be about man's inability to communicate with other humans. Obviously, you've given much thought to this matter.

GILMOUR Well, it was never really a conscious decision to take it on as a theme—it just happened. One or two things started to move in that direction, and as soon as a theme begins to appear I find it very hard to get away from.

GW Do you find that you need a theme to get the creative juices flowing?

GILMOUR I don't think so. Usually, though, one eventually appears in my work. Something comes up that ties the whole thing together. Your mood at the time of making and writing an album usually supplies the subject matter. In the past I have tried to sit down and consciously create a concept, but it never seemed to work very well. It has to appear naturally. And it has to be kind of nebulous—something that's come up of its own volition.

GW Like most Floyd albums, *The Division Bell* has a universal theme. But it also seems more intimate than your past work. Were you trying to create something more personal?

GILMOUR I wasn't trying to. Again, all I can really say is that it is just the way it seemed to come up. It probably had something to do with "High Hopes," my first composition for the album. The song originated from a phrase that my girlfriend suggested, about how time brings you down. Oddly, the line that she gave me wasn't really important. There was just something in it that sparked me into thinking about my childhood and my life in Cambridge, England. So, if you like, the first thing that got written for the album was much more personal than I've tended to be. And I suppose it set the scene for what was to follow.

GW Was recording the album cathartic for you?

GILMOUR No. I don't really think so. I can't really say that there was a huge angst that needed to be purged through songwriting. It wasn't like *The Wall*. But, on the other hand, maybe I did need to unload my subconscious. It just never really struck me that way.

GW Several songs on the album, like "Keep Talking," suggest that all problems can be solved through discussion. Do you believe that?

GILMOUR It's more of a wish than a belief. [*laughs*]

GW Do you find it difficult to express your feelings verbally?

GILMOUR Yes, I do, I suppose. I mean, I have moments of huge frustration because of my inability to express myself linguistically as clearly as I would like to. A lot of people think that I express myself most clearly through the guitar playing. I don't know about that. But it's just...I don't like that feeling of frustration when you don't quite have the words to say what you want to say.

GW You collaborated with other lyricists on *The Division Bell*. Was that to help you express your ideas more clearly?

GILMOUR Well, a lot of the lyrics were the result of a collaboration between myself and my girlfriend, Polly Samson. She's a journalist and writer. After I would write some lyrics, it just seemed natural to have her look through them. In the beginning she tried not to interfere at all, and tried to encourage me to do it on my own. Of course, that isn't the way things stay. And as time went by, she got more and more involved with the process that was beginning to absorb me 24 hours a day. Her involvement with the lyric-writing process—and, in fact, with the music—grew. It's been really nice to work with Polly and have input from someone who never wanted to write a pop song. And I imagine it was very good for her to realize that her brain could actually function musically, although she has no musical skill whatsoever. Her assistance was invaluable.

GW A musical novice can often see something that would elude a trained musician.

GILMOUR That's right.

GW The album has a lot to do with people's failure to communicate, so it must have been interesting to discuss those kinds of barriers with someone you're close to. Did it help your relationship?

GILMOUR Oh, of course. Some of the lyrics actually came out of our relationship. And some, unfortunately, came after moments where there was a lack of communication between us. For example, the title "What Do You Want from Me?" came out of exactly one of those moments.

GW It doesn't surprise me that the record has a more emotional vibe than those where the lyrics were written primarily by Roger Waters. [*Bassist/composer Waters left Floyd in 1985, citing creative and philosophical disagreements.*] Your guitar playing has always been Pink Floyd's emotional anchor.

GILMOUR It has been said. And I would agree with that.

GW Did you discover anything about yourself as you were going through the process of writing and working on this record?

GILMOUR [*slightly annoyed*] I don't know what I've discovered about myself, really. No, I don't. I haven't a clue. What was really nice about the recording of this record was that Rick [*Wright, keyboardist*] and Nick [*Mason, drummer*] and I came together and worked well as a unit in a way that we hadn't done for many, many years. Additionally, I discovered another separate creative team—a lyric-writing team consisting of me, Polly and my close friend Nick Laird-Clowes. And although there were two separate teams, *The Division Bell* does feel like a very cohesive record. It feels like we all meant it and like we all played together very well. And the whole thing is very much a joint effort—in a much greater way than, for example, the last album, *A Momentary Lapse of Reason.*

GW Why are you relating better to Nick and Rick?

GILMOUR Probably because we are all playing and functioning much better than we were after the trials and tribulations of the late Roger years. Recording *A Momentary Lapse of Reason* was a very, very difficult process. We were all sort of catatonic. Unfortunately, we didn't really work together an awful lot.

But the success of that album, and the success of the supporting tour and the enjoyment that we got out of working together—particularly on the last tour—meant that this one could be made in a different way. It's a much more satisfying way to work than the way *A Momentary Lapse of Reason* came together. Yeah, they're very different albums.

GW Does it feel like a new band for you?

GILMOUR It feels like a good start. It feels like there's better things to come. I'm really, really happy and very proud of this album.

GW There was a long period between this and the last studio album. Why?

GILMOUR It's just that we didn't feel like working. I don't want to

Larry Busacca/Retna

A Water-less Pink Floyd is inducted into the Rock and Roll Hall of Fame, 1996. (*Left-to-right*): David Gilmour, Nick Mason, Richard Wright.

be a full-time member of Pink Floyd all my life. The ambition stage of our career is kind of behind us. I mean, we've accomplished most of the things we've wanted to accomplish. It's now just a pleasure to make a record. But it's still very hard to get yourself psyched up and motivated to do it. Pink Floyd is now one of many other things in my life. You earn the right—and we *have* earned the right—to take time off. When you're starting out on a career, you don't have that luxury. You have to devote every minute of every day in every year to work. You just have to work so hard and so consistently to make a career out of this business that we're in. And for me, I just don't have to do it quite as much.

GW Although the album clearly makes a personal statement, it also contains some specific political statements. On "A Great Day for Freedom," for instance, you address the great hopes triggered by the fall of the Berlin Wall, and the disappointment that followed in Europe.

GILMOUR Yeah. Well, it's kind of tragic what has happened in the eastern parts of Europe. There was a wonderful moment of optimism when the Wall came down—the release of Eastern Europe from the non-democratic side of the socialist system. But what they have now doesn't seem to be much better. Again, I'm fairly pessimistic about it all. I sort of wish and live in hope, but I tend to think that history moves at a much slower pace than we think it does. I feel that real change takes a long, long time. We see the superficial changes that people think are enormous. But they pass, and several years down the road you find yourself back at the same place you were 20 years before, thinking, My God, all of this happened and nothing happened.

GW "Lost for Words" also reflects a certain pessimism. The lyrics read, "So I open my door to my enemies/And I ask could we wipe the slate clean/But they tell me to please go fuck myself/You know you just can't win." What do you do when somebody just tells you to go fuck yourself?

GILMOUR Well, the options are immediate. [*laughs*] You can simply become a good contortionist—there's one option. Or just deck him. Or talk the matter out.

GW At what point do you think a relationship is no longer worth pursuing?

GILMOUR I don't know if that's something I can put into words. But it seems that I'm usually prepared to stick it out a lot longer than what, in hindsight, one should.

GW The album ends with a funny little studio snippet of you talking to a little boy named Charlie. It seems to suggest that the potential for miscommunication spans generations.

GILMOUR That is pretty succinct. [*laughs*]

GW At the same time, you must find it interesting that your music has multigenerational appeal. I saw people of all ages at your show.

GILMOUR It does really surprise me. But I think that we do have sort of a timeless quality. I listened to *Dark Side of the Moon* last year around the time of the release of our *Shine On* box set, and I remember feeling that it was pretty timeless. And a lot of the issues that we have dealt with—that Roger wrote about in his lyrics, if you like—are pretty timeless. They are things that apply to any generation.

GW The band's success stems from the fact that it confronts ideas that have puzzled men from Day One.

GILMOUR Well, I'm certainly still a puzzled man. [*laughs*]

GW How involved are you with the staging of the band?

GILMOUR We were constantly involved during the entire process of designing and building the stage. Lots of things got turned down. And we wound up with the sort of thing that we all agree is good.

GW You said earlier that you prefer not to explain the meaning of your lyrics, but in the staging of shows past and present you have used lots of very literal props to illustrate your ideas: flying pigs, crashing airplanes, collapsing walls...

GILMOUR Yes. Yes. [*laughs*] That's true. But I think this show is a little less literal and more impressionistic. It's a little less flashy, and because of that I'm probably more satisfied with this tour than any we've done.

GW Let's talk about the live show a little bit. I noticed that you began each set with a little tribute to Syd Barrett. [*Barrett, Pink Floyd's founding singer/guitarist, left the band in 1968 due to mental illness.*] The first set leads off with Syd's "Astronomy Domine," and the second set opens with "Shine On You Crazy Diamond," which makes allusions to Syd. Am I reading too much into this?

GILMOUR I think so. It wasn't a conscious decision to pay homage to Syd. We've probably paid homage to him quite enough. [*laughs*] We basically just wanted to widen the spectrum a little bit and find one or two pieces of music we haven't done before. "Astronomy" just struck us as being a very good opening number. It's fun to go back and do that, despite some of the lyrics—it's hard to sing it with a straight face. And "Shine On" was a terrific opener for the last tour, so now we just use it to open the second half of the show.

GW It must cross your mind, from time to time, how your life would be different if you hadn't replaced Syd in the band. Do you feel indebted to him at all?

GILMOUR Yes, of course, I do. I feel a debt to Syd. I was very fortunate. His bad luck was good luck for me. Of course, one can not possibly know what would have happened. Luckily, I don't have to ponder that too deeply. [*laughs*]

GW Your particular relationship with stardom is a little peculiar. You front one of the most popular bands in the world, yet you've managed to keep a low profile. You're modest almost to a perverse point. For example, during your solo for "Comfortably Numb," which is one of the highlights of the concert, the laser show directs the audience away from you.

GILMOUR That is a little perverse. But it's a two-and-a-half-hour show, and I think I get more adoration than I probably deserve. So I can't really worry about the odd moments when people are watching something else.

GW Are there moments in the show that you really look forward to?

GILMOUR I enjoy the newer material. At the same time, I realize that you have to achieve a balance between playing all the stuff that you'd want to play and playing stuff that you know the audience wants to hear. I don't harbor any resentment against the audience for wanting to hear our older material. They aren't making value judgments. They're more familiar with the older songs and how they are connected to moments in their lives.

GW Let's talk about your guitar playing on some of the new songs. "What Do You Want from Me?" is a straight Chicago blues tune. Are you still a blues fan?

GILMOUR Absolutely—even though I don't listen to very much blues anymore. I did listen to quite a lot when I was young. But I also listened to a lot of folk music and a lot of everything else.

GW Your blues influence is obvious, but I do hear a lot of folky, hymnlike overtones on some of your quieter songs like "On the Turning Away," "Wish You Were Here" and "Poles Apart."

GILMOUR I actually learned the guitar with the help of a Pete Seeger [*folk legend and writer of "Turn, Turn, Turn"*] instructional record when I was 13 or 14. And I did listen to a lot of folk and folk-blues. [*African American folk singer*] Leadbelly and Pete Seeger were both big influences on me.

GW I also hear some Bob Dylan in your music.

GILMOUR I actually saw his first-ever show in England when I was about 15. Bob is about as good as it gets. People tend to think of him as just a lyricist, but he is actually a brilliant composer, as well, and a great singer—brilliant singer, yeah, fabulous!

GW Have you ever wanted to see what you could do with one of Dylan's songs?

GILMOUR I have, actually. I've had some fun mucking about in my home studio with things like a reggae version of "Like a Rolling Stone."

GW What can you tell me about *The Division Bell*'s guitar instrumental, "Marooned"?

GILMOUR It's amazing how far I can bend those notes, isn't it? [*laughs*]

GW I'll say. How did you achieve those wild, octave-wide bends?

GILMOUR A DigiTech Whammy Pedal. It's a great little unit, but I haven't even begun to explore half the things it does. The fact that it allows you to bend a note a full octave is quite shocking. It's so odd.

GW You seem to use the effect very naturally—I almost didn't notice it at first. Did you practice with it a lot before you recorded "Marooned"?

GILMOUR No. [*laughs*] I think we basically wrote the first version of it the day I got the pedal. I still don't think I use it very effectively, but it's a good pedal.

GW How much of "Marooned" is improvised?

GILMOUR Pretty much all of it. I probably took three or four passes at it and took the best bits out of each.

GW Do you experiment much with your guitar in the studio?

GILMOUR Not really. My guitar tech, Phil Taylor, tries to make me experiment much more than I would if I were left to my own devices. If I've got an amp or a couple of amps, and a guitar that I like, I'll just do everything with those. I'm very low-tech when it comes to effects. I tend to still use pedals like the Big Muff. I'm not a fan of rack units—they don't have any balls to them. I still like my grungey old pedals. Most of what I use can be found in any music store anywhere.

GW Did you use an EBow on "Take It Back"?

GILMOUR Yeah! On a Gibson J-200 acoustic guitar that is processed through a Zoom effects box, then directly injected into the board.

GW That's a pretty bizarre configuration.

GILMOUR Well, I guess I experiment more than I think I do! I had a Zoom in my control room one day, and I was mucking about with something. Suddenly, I thought I should stick the EBow on the strings and see what would happen. It sounded great, so we started writing a little duet for the EBowed acoustic guitar and a keyboard. We never finished the piece, but [*keyboardist*] Jon Carin decided to sample the EBowed guitar part. We kept the sample and ended up using it as a loop on "Take It Back" and again on "Keep Talking."

GW How do you achieve that spacious Pink Floyd sound?

GILMOUR Of course we try to do everything as well as we possibly can. We have to get a reasonably good recording studio. And you need to get nice tape machines and pretty good mikes. You get the best engineer that you can lay your hands on. And, of course, you play it as well as you can. And that's it. It seems kind of odd to me that we should have the reputation of being "high tech." I mean, I actually once got a little award from a stereo magazine for my production on the first Dream Academy album [The Dream Academy, *Warner Bros., 1985*]. What was amusing to me was that the album was actually made in small demo studios all over London. We just worked and mixed the hell out of it. I couldn't believe that we really got this award. I have to admit, it does sound very good. But if you knew the way it was put together, you couldn't imagine that we would win an audiophile award.

GW What people might not realize is that your spacious sound has something to do with your arrangements.

GILMOUR I would agree. I have always had a 3D sound in my head. I like to have some element of space and depth in everything we do; I can't seem to get away from that. And I listen to a lot of records and find them two-dimensional, just in the way they're mixed. And the sad part is that it's not hard to add dimension.

GW Can you give me a specific example of how you spice up a typical Pink Floyd production?

GILMOUR The EBow loop in "Take It Back" is a good example. If you take that off it becomes a totally different song. That relatively simple effect adds a whole extra dimension of space to the song.

GW How was this recording experience different from those of the past?

GILMOUR It was not that different. We used less sequencing this time than we did last time. We played more music in real time.

GW When you're working with Nick and Rick on the initial ideas, is there a lot of verbal communication?

GILMOUR Not much. Initially, we spent about three weeks just jamming and throwing ideas around. I recorded anything that started sounding remotely interesting on a small stereo DAT machine. Then we went back to the studio, listened and logged everything in. In total there were about 65 little pieces of music, and that was the start for us. And it was a very good start. These days I do less and less demoing for songs. I tend to just record ideas on a simple cassette recorder, using only an acoustic guitar—something very, very rough. And then I don't record the idea again until I'm playing it well enough to commit it to a proper machine. The worst thing is to record a crummy demo that has that great atmosphere to it and then spend months and months trying to recreate it. This is exactly what happened, in fact, on "High Hopes." I did a complete demo of that in a day at the studio. But for some reason we couldn't use it because, I think, maybe the tempo wavered a little bit. It then took ages to capture a take that was anywhere near as good as the demo. It was the first song written for the album, and the last one finished.

GW I noticed that you use a D A D G A D tuning on "Poles Apart." That's a new tuning for you.

GILMOUR Yes, but the funny thing is that I didn't know it was such an established tuning—I thought it was something new that I had invented. One day I was on holiday in Greece and I had an acoustic guitar with me. I just decided to tune the bottom string down to D, and continued to experiment until I arrived at that tuning. Then I mucked around a bit and "Poles Apart" fell out of it a few minutes later.

GW Why do you use a lap steel on songs like "High Hopes" and "Great Gig in the Sky" instead of playing straight slide guitar on your Strat?

GILMOUR I always had a fondness for pedal steels and lap steels. I guess it's because I could never come to grips with standard bottleneck playing.

GW You have two Fender lap steels on tour with you. How are they tuned?

GILMOUR The one that I use on "High Hopes" is tuned to a first-position E minor chord. The other one, which I use on "Great Gig in the Sky," is tuned like a regular guitar except for the top two strings—D G D G B E. That allows me to form a minor chord on the top three strings and a major chord with all the other strings.

GW Do you feel like you're improving as a musician, as a guitarist?

GILMOUR I don't really know. I doubt if I'm improving very much as a guitar player. If I sound better these days, I think it has more to do with the wonders of modern recording techniques and with having my own studio. Having your own studio often means having the luxury to keep first takes, which are usually my best. And most of the guitar playing on this album is literally the first time I stuck a guitar on and played. In the old days, I usually wasn't able to keep the first take. We either didn't have the tape machine on, or I gave my best shot in a rehearsal room somewhere. So to answer your question: no, I'm not getting better as a guitarist, but I think I'm better at capturing the good moments and hanging on to them.

GW It does seem to me that, guitar-wise, this is a very ambitious record. Sonically, almost every song has something a little different to offer.

GILMOUR I'm glad someone thinks so. [*laughs*] Lots of people think we're merely retreading old ground.

Guitar World, September 1995

Mooney Tunes

Pink Floyd highlighted their 1994 tour with performances, for the first time in decades, of their classic *Dark Side of the Moon* album. David Gilmour offers his take on *Pulse*, the band's document of that historic tour.

By Gary Graff

The booklet that accompanies Pink Floyd's new live album, *Pulse*, includes a photo of guitarist David Gilmour juggling some plastic cups while bandmates Nick Mason and Rick Wright look on. Gilmour says he's not much of a juggler; it was just an end-of-tour prank, when a crew member dumped a box of cups on the band. "We actually cut that person out of the picture," Gilmour says with a chuckle, "just to show him what he gets for messing with us."

As an image, however, the photo is a fine metaphor for the work Gilmour has done in the 10 years since he assumed control of Pink Floyd following Roger Waters' tempestuous departure. During that time, the 48-year-old Gilmour has juggled all sorts of elements and responsibilities. He put together a new Pink Floyd, drawing Mason and Wright out of creative catatonia and recruiting an additional cadre of young musicians. He stood up to Waters' assault on the band in the courts and in the media, rebuffing his former bandmate and former writing partner's notion that Pink Floyd was invalid without him.

Most importantly, Gilmour led Pink Floyd to two new albums and two enormously successful world tours. And he returned the group to a particularly high creative stature; their album of last year,

The Division Bell, was not only a compelling work but also the work of a band—unlike 1987's *A Momentary Lapse of Reason*, which was the product of a Gilmour-led committee.

All of this helped make the visually overwhelming and sonically powerful 1994 tour an absolute triumph. *Pulse*—which features *Dark Side of the Moon* performed in its entirety, along with 14 other Floyd favorites—preserves the spirit of the event; the blinking red LED light on the package even provides a nod to the show's feast of lasers, lighting majesty, pyrotechnics and special effects.

To mark the album's release, Gilmour pulled himself away from his hearth and infant child to reminisce about the tour and make some noncommittal predictions about Pink Floyd's future.

GUITAR WORLD Did you expect to record a live album during the last tour?

DAVID GILMOUR No, we didn't. We did one just a few years ago, for the *Momentary Lapse of Reason* tour. We never thought we'd do one again this soon. But when we got out on the road and started thinking about what we could do differently this time, different tunes we hadn't played before and things like that, we said, "Why don't we try putting *Dark Side of the Moon* back together?" It seemed like a pretty fair idea.

So we hunted down all the bits of old film and quadraphonic tape, and got some new bits of film together because some of that old stuff had gotten damaged or was out of date. Obviously, it took a while to get all that together while we were busy playing and touring.

By the end of the American part of the tour, we'd just about gotten everything together. We played it two or three times in America, and that was such a good feeling. We decided that we'd like to have a copy of it live, and we thought other people would want to have a copy of it live, too. We started thinking about just putting out *Dark Side of the Moon* live, then decided, screw it, we'll just give them the whole show again.

GW Whose idea was it to put the flashing LED light on the spine of the CD box?

GILMOUR That was Storm Thorgerson, from Hipgnosis; those are our old people who have designed most of our album covers. They've done a lot of the film stuff we've used onstage, too. In addition to the music it contained, he wanted the album package itself to have a live element. It's also, happily, a sort of visual reminder of the heartbeat at the beginning of *Dark Side of the Moon*.

GW What made you decide to do *Dark Side* again?

GILMOUR Really, just a desire to do something different; it wasn't an anniversary or anything like that. The fact is we were doing half to two-thirds of the *Dark Side* tunes already—"Money," "The Great Gig in the Sky," "Breathe"—so that left us with only three or four pieces we weren't doing. We thought it would be quite a simple operation to get ready and do it, though it actually took months. Obviously, we wouldn't have done a live album of this tour had we not been doing *Dark Side*.

GW When was the last time you performed the entire *Dark Side*?

GILMOUR We hadn't really played it since 1975. We were kind of sorry we never recorded it live, or filmed it. It was a great show back then. So we did discuss it with Roger [*Waters*], as we were getting more and more grumpy with each other. We said we should put together *Dark Side* just so we had it on film for posterity.

As I said, on our last tour, we were already playing most of the album, so we just had to pick up the instrumental package, "Any Colour You Like," then "Brain Damage" and "Eclipse." They are the two songs which Roger sang the lead part on on the original record, which is one of the reasons we avoided them before.

GW How did you feel singing them?

GILMOUR It was a little nerve-wracking doing Roger's vocal parts the first time. But it went down well. Detroit [*where the revived* Dark Side *debuted*] was a real high, emotional moment.

GW *Pulse* seems to capture the band in a more relaxed state than you've been in the past. Was that the case?

GILMOUR It was. It was much more relaxed. In '87, it was our first album without Roger, our first tour without Roger, our first tour with all these new musicians. We were kind of nervous, and up against it a little bit. This time it was totally relaxed. The musicians all knew how to be Pink Floyd, for starters.

And we managed to get away from some of the computer stuff we used on the previous tour. Everything was more open to spontaneity. We had a system where we could change the set half an hour before we went on. That made the whole thing more open to a looser, more spontaneous feel, which I feel comes out on the record.

GW How often did you change things around?

GILMOUR Most shows. We'd say, "Let's put a different song in the first half. Let's change the order around a little bit." After Detroit, we'd throw *Dark Side* in sometimes. We changed the set nearly every night to keep ourselves on the ball and interested.

GW Did this effect your guitar playing at all?

GILMOUR God, someone else would have to tell me that. I just play the thing; I certainly wasn't thinking all that much. Every night I'm just trying to find something new to play.

GW Your soloing throughout the tour was pretty inspired, which comes across on *Pulse*.

GILMOUR It just goes along with the whole vibe thing we've discussed—the more relaxed, looser sort of approach. I was certainly enjoying myself on the gigs; if that came across, I cannot be anything but pleased.

GW You played "Astronomy Domine," too, which was a surprising nod to Floyd's distant past.

GILMOUR Again, we had done pretty much everything we liked and wanted to do and thought we were capable of doing on the '87 tour. On this tour, we wanted to have a change, try some songs we hadn't done before. So we hunted through all the records, and someone suggested we try "Astronomy Domine." We also did "Hey You," which we didn't do on the previous tour. And we changed "Shine On You Crazy Diamond" around a little bit.

GW It probably made a difference that *The Division Bell* was really more of a band project than *A Momentary Lapse of Reason.*

GILMOUR It was. The way we put together the *Division Bell* album was by jamming in the studio—just myself, Rick and Nick, with Guy [*Pratt*] on bass. It heralded a return to the older way of doing things, if you like.

GW Much of the material on *The Division Bell* had a sad, melancholy aura about it. How are you feeling these days?

GILMOUR Fine, really. It's just that the sadder, more difficult things tend to be better themes for music. They tend to be easier to come to grips with. Doing happy, cheerful songs is tougher. But I'm not in a miserable state at all. I have a new baby boy; I'm a happy man, truly.

GW Why was everybody's confidence so low back in '87?

GILMOUR It's a long, old story about Roger and the last few years of his reign. He had really sapped all the confidence out of Rick and Nick; they didn't feel they were up to the job anymore. It took the last tour, in '87 and '88, to get them back into shape, to get back the confidence and self-esteem.

GW Is all the Roger stuff behind you now?

GILMOUR It would be if people didn't keep asking me about it. The fact is that the last thing we did together was the *Final Cut* album, in 1982—13 years ago. Roger officially left in '85, 10 years ago. I can't be dealing with it; it's long in the past, forgotten for me.

Of course, people keep asking me about it. I don't want to say anything that would reduce Roger's stature within his time in the band. Obviously, we had some very successful projects. He was a great lyric writer, and I have nothing but respect for his abilities. But times change, and you move on and you make your choices. He left us with no option. It's not something I spend my time being obsessed by.

GW Is there any contact at all—besides sending him his royalty checks?

GILMOUR Not much. He did give us permission to put out the *Dark Side of the Moon* stuff on video; you have to have the writer's permission to get a synchronization license to put out a video. But that's about it, as far as contact goes.

GW The '94 tour set all sorts of attendance and revenue records. Can you take it for granted that Pink Floyd is able to do that each time out?

GILMOUR I think we can assume that people are going to listen to us. If they like it, we'll sell some records. But you can't assume anything. *The Wall* album was one of our real high spots; we sold countless copies of that. But the album immediately following that, *The Final Cut*, really didn't sell so great. People don't just rush out and buy things; they listen first, I think.

GW Have you been working on any new songs?

GILMOUR I write bits of songs constantly. We also have many bits of music we didn't get to use on the last album. Some of it's terrific, so there's no shortage of start-off spots. We will get there one of these days. I think Rick is working on a solo album or something, and Nick is writing his own book about Pink Floyd.

GW So will we have to wait seven years for the next studio album?

GILMOUR Maybe. [*laughs*] I don't know. I've been too busy with family life and putting together the live album and video to even think about the future. But we'll get there; when, I'm afraid I don't know myself.

GW What do you know about this Publius character on the Internet?

GILMOUR I know nothing whatsoever. People keep asking me questions about it, but I'm actually not on the Internet. I haven't seen the stuff. I was told people are hunting for something, but I don't know what it is.

GW Apparently, words like "Enigma Publius" appeared in your lighting and projections during the tour, giving the appearance that the band is somehow involved.

GILMOUR I can't see the lights where I am. [*laughs*] I know a lot of our lighting guys are on the computer, on the Internet. Maybe they join in with the rumor. I've been meaning to get on the Internet, but I haven't quite managed to get around to it. I did get enrolled on a system, but my old laptop didn't seem to do the job.

GW There's some talk of Pink Floyd showing up to play at the Rock and Roll Hall of Fame opening in September. Any truth to that?

GILMOUR Not that I know of. We were nominated for induction a couple of years ago, and they turned us down. I'll think about it when they ask, but I honestly haven't thought much about it. When we were in Cleveland, they asked us to go down to the building and see it. I got grumpy and said no, I wasn't going to. They'd just turned me down for induction; why should I go there if they didn't want me?

GW Do you listen to much in the way of modern rock?

GILMOUR I heard a new Van Morrison song yesterday on the radio; that leaped out to me as, "Hmmm, this is something of quality." Not much does these days. I've been impressed by one or two Lemonheads songs, some PJ Harvey songs. The new Marianne Faithfull sounds good, but that's hardly young. I like unusual things, I guess. I'm not a great Pearl Jam fan.

Guitar World, February 1998

The Eye of the Storm

Visionary designer Storm Thorgerson looks back at 30 years of landmark album art for Led Zeppelin, Genesis, Phish and, of course, Pink Floyd.

By Gary Graff

"**G**uitar World? What kind of magazine is that?"

The questioner is Storm Thorgerson. He doesn't play guitar. In fact, he claims he doesn't even know "one end of the guitar from another."

So what's he doing here? As one of the three partners in Hipgnosis, once the preeminent and most visionary album art design firm in the world, Thorgerson has put his stamp on rock and roll history via photographs, illustrations and ambitious packaging for some of rock's landmark albums. Works by Pink Floyd, Led Zeppelin, Paul McCartney, Yes, Wishbone Ash, John McLaughlin, Genesis and many others bear the stamp of Thorgerson and Hipgnosis, which disbanded in 1983.

Thorgerson has continued to work as an in-demand album designer—two of his most recent clients have been Dream Theater and Phish—and video director. That he remains so highly sought-after is hardly surprising. Any working musician who once sorted seeds from weed in the gatefold of one of his classic creations would probably be thrilled to see Thorgerson have his ethereal way with an album of theirs.

"He's awesome," says John Petrucci of Dream Theater, for whom Thorgerson designed the cover of *Falling into Infinity*. "We've always wanted to work with him. In the past we would actually sketch our album covers ourselves, then get together with the people who would execute them. This time around, Storm insisted on doing the whole thing, and we just deferred. When you're working with someone of that caliber, you can trust his professional instincts."

No band has trusted Thorgerson more during the past 30 years than Pink Floyd, whose relationship with the designer dates back nearly five decades to Cambridge, England, where Thorgerson grew up with Floyd's original band leader Syd Barrett, who was a year behind him in school, and former bassist Roger Waters, who was a year ahead. Thorgerson and Waters played rugby together.

They went their separate ways in college, but everyone wound up in swinging London during the mid Sixties, as rock and roll culture took over the city. Starting with *A Saucerful of Secrets* in 1968, Thorgerson became Pink Floyd's chief album designer, crafting a series of indelible images—the picture-within-a-picture cover of *Ummagumma*, the cow of *Atom Heart Mother*, the prism of *Dark Side of the Moon*, the Easter Island-style totems of *The Division Bell*.

Beyond the albums, there were videos and concert films, as well as covers for solo projects by Gilmour and Barrett. With the notable exceptions of *The Wall*, *The Final Cut* and a handful of other releases, Thorgerson was responsible for the visual face of Pink Floyd. He'd blanch at any reference to him as the band's fifth member, but in Floyd's extra-musical domain, it was Thorgerson's vision that set the controls for the heart of the sun.

"He has been my friend, my conscience, my therapist and of course my artistic advisor...," Gilmour writes in the foreword of *Mind over Matter: The Images of Pink Floyd* (Sanctuary Music Library), a 176-page tour of the incredible graphic world Thorgerson has created for the band. "Storm's ideas are not linked to anyone's ideas of marketing: that they are atmospherically linked to the music is a bonus. I consider what he does to be art."

Gilmour also notes with obvious affection that "Storm has always had a big mouth," an observation confirmed by the designer during a long conversation in his London office, in which he generously shares his thoughts about Floyd, Zeppelin, his myriad other projects and the general state of album art. All this, of course, after he is assured that "the fact that I don't know anything about guitars doesn't disqualify me from being in *Guitar World*, is that right?"

GUITAR WORLD How did your association with Pink Floyd begin?

STORM THORGERSON It began with Syd, but also with Roger. Roger's mom and my mum were best friends. Also with Dave, because he used to hang around with us, even though he was younger. It was just a gang in Cambridge…a group of teenagers who came together, not unlike, I should think, they do in many places in America. Roger was more on the fringes of our peer group; we both chased the same girl…but he won that one.

GW What were the Floyd guys like as teens? Ordinary, red-blooded young English lads?

THORGERSON I think that Roger and Syd were not that ordinary…or the others, for that matter. They have ordinary things they do in their lives—they're not absolutely weird as hell—and they have the usual set of passions. They also make the usual number of mistakes that us normal people do. But they also have drive and talent, obviously. And also, in some cases, great musicianship. I think Dave lent them a sense of musicianship that helped them to be very successful.

GW What was it like, watching the band come together?

THORGERSON I didn't see it. I went off to another university. They came to architectural school in London, and Dave joined later, anyway. I didn't do the first album; I didn't do *Piper at the Gates of Dawn*. I knew them, and I knew they were being nearly successful. But although I knew them as friends, I didn't have a particular view of this, other than it was exciting to know a band that might be successful. I didn't pay too much attention; I was too preoccupied with myself, as one is when one is younger. When I met them again, they were in the process of losing Syd. So their main creative talent was sort of going off the rails. It's hard to find the correct way to describe it, really.

GW In Nicholas Schaffner's book *A Saucerful of Secrets*, he describes a meeting in your apartment where Syd's ouster from the band was discussed. What was that like?

THORGERSON It's a bit long ago to remember. [*laughs*] Because they knew that I knew Syd, and I knew them, they thought maybe I could perhaps offer some limited advice as to what to do. Rog, who hadn't spoken to me in quite a bit, I think was interested in talking to me about what I thought was going wrong with Syd, 'cause he knew that I'd been relatively close to him in Cambridge. But I don't think that I had much of an idea about what they should do, really. It's very difficult, even when you're an adult, to know what to do when a friend goes off the rails. It was very hard for the band; I don't think there was ever a desire to get rid of him, but they had to function.

We talked about it, as chaps do. I couldn't proffer much direct advice, but we chatted about how horribly difficult it was, what the hell they were going to do. Syd was in such a state at times, you just couldn't talk to him. I think I was of the opinion then that it made sense to get rid of him if he really was preventing the band from functioning. He seemed to show clear signs of getting worse rather than better, and also seemed to be unreachable. If a person seems unreachable, or appears to be immune to entreaty, then you have to reluctantly decide to go on without him.

I think it's very sad, really. And they were very sad about it. I think "Shine On You Crazy Diamond" is the most concretized form of their sadness, if you like. I think that song, written eight years later, approximately, is a clear indication that this was something they did not want to happen.

GW So in the midst of this, you wound up doing the art for *A Saucerful of Secrets*.

THORGERSON I think they knew they didn't want the record company to handle it. This was in the days when the Floyd and the Stones and the Beatles were beginning to take power back to themselves, especially artistic power, away from the record companies—to literally take more control of their artistic output. I think they realized that, along with the music, sleeves are things that last, and that maybe they're important in their own way. Even if they're not as important as the music, except to people like me.

I think they wanted someone they trusted and who knew them to do it rather than some impersonal or third-party designer that had no relationship with them. Their music was intimately related; why shouldn't their cover be related?

GW So what if you hadn't liked the music?

THORGERSON [*laughs*] I didn't think particularly in those terms. I was keen to do it. I don't know that I applied much critical faculty to the question of whether the music was really good or not. I think I just thought it was all really great. You have to remember the Floyd were extremely cutting edge and contemporary. It was all terribly exciting. So I think I was carried along in that wave, really.

GW What kind of working relationship did you fall into with the band?

THORGERSON You get used to each other and you chat and you develop some shorthands. And you prick your ears to pick up the bits that are most interesting. *Dark Side*, for example, came from sort of an aside said by Rick—not necessarily the most likely source. The back of *Ummagumma* comes from something Nick Mason did. *Meddle* comes from God knows what. *Wish You Were Here* comes from conversations with Rog in particular. *Animals* is actually a Roger thing; although we did the work, it was his idea. *A Momentary Lapse of Reason* comes from a line of lyric of Dave's. *The Division Bell* comes from several things.

What happens is, in all these cases, you still have a sort of communication with the band. That comes and goes. It breaks down sometimes. It's mostly by talking, by being there—by going to gigs, particularly, so that you get some sensation of what the music is really like, 'cause you don't find that much during recording, since a lot of it is done in bits.

GW Is it important to start working on the album art at the gestation of the project?

THORGERSON It depends on what the gestation was. I didn't have anything, really, to do with the start of *Atom Heart Mother*, and when I asked them what it was about, they said they didn't know themselves. It's a conglomeration of pieces that weren't related, or didn't seem to be at the time. The picture isn't related either; in fact, it was an attempt to do a picture that was unrelated, consciously unrelated.

GW It's a cow!

THORGERSON 'Cause that seemed to be the most unrelated thing it could be. Also, I think the cow represents, in terms of the Pink

Floyd, part of their humor, which I think is often underestimated or just unwritten about. Not that their music is funny, but I think they have good senses of humor. Nick is very droll; he's got a very good dry sense of humor. And Roger is very sharp. Dave has his own particular sense of humor, as well. I think that's why they chose the cow. I think they thought it was funny.

GW Any rejections of your work that come readily to mind?

THORGERSON Yeah, for *Animals* in particular. There were two roughs for *Animals,* one of which was a picture of a young child, age three or four, with a teddy bear, opening the room to his parents, who are on the bed making love, being caught in the act, and appearing to be animals. I thought that was really good, but they didn't like it.

For the same job, I also suggested this idea about ducks. In England, the essence of bad taste is to put plaster ducks on the wall. So I took that idea and put real ducks and nailed them to the wall to suggest that people are really animal in some of their artistic and moral decisions. I think they rejected that not because they didn't like it—because I think they did—but because it was very heavy. These were ducks I bought at a poultry place and nailed to a wall.

So yeah, it happens. For *Dark Side of the Moon,* we did six or seven complex roughs of all sorts of different things that were eminently suitable. And we were very excited and looking forward to showing these different ideas to the band. At the actual meeting, we gathered around and…it took about a minute! They looked at all these things and looked at the prism and said, "We'll have that." We said, "Oh, there's this and this, have a look at this." And they said, "No, we'll have that. Now we've got to go back and do our real job." And they walked out of the room to continue recording.

GW While *Dark Side* was being recorded, was there a sense that it was a special album?

THORGERSON Not that I remember. I think they thought they'd made a pretty good record, but not "mega," to use their term. I think they were unbelievably surprised at its reception and gratified, and continue to be so. I mean, it changed their lives.

GW You tell a great story in the book about shooting the pyramids in the middle of the night for the *Dark Side* poster.

THORGERSON I scared myself shitless doing it, too! I hired a taxi at 2 o'clock a.m. to take me out to the pyramids. So there I am, thinking I'll be fine, and I put the camera on the tripod to do a long-time exposure. It's a wonderful, clear night, and the moon is fantastic. So I'm doing it … and then, at like 4 o'clock a.m., these figures come walking across—soldiers, with guns. I thought, This is it. The game is up—young photographer dies a strange death in a foreign land. I was actually really scared. Of course, all my fears were unfounded. They were very friendly. They wanted a bit of bakshish, a little bit of money to go away. They kindly pointed out that where I stood was actually a firing range, and that they'd come to tell me it wasn't very cool for me to be there. If I was there first thing in the morning, I might get a bullet up my butt.

GW It's obvious from the book that you're very fond of *Wish You Were Here*. Did you feel you had to one-up *Dark Side*?

THORGERSON Not really. *Dark Side* … I think it's sort of goodish, good. Sort of. But I don't think it's a moving piece; I don't think it's as moving as I would like in terms of their music. So when *Wish You Were Here* came around, I was quite fueled up for it. In fact, I was even more fueled up for it. And I only suggested one thing to them, as opposed to several to choose from. It was quite nervy, 'cause normally for the Floyd and other bands I would suggest a few different roughs to choose from. But the one thing that was suggested to the band was what they used.

GW Those images were mostly inspired by "Shine On You Crazy Diamond," correct?

THORGERSON It was particularly to do with "Shine On You Crazy Diamond," yes. In a way, that theme could be expressed by one word: absence. It was absence in terms of relationships, absence in terms of previous members of the band. Also, absence in terms of a commitment to a cause or a project. This was a feeling that I think was in the air.

GW How involved did you get in those inner-band Floyd politics that started to surface during the mid Seventies?

THORGERSON The divorce, you mean? Quite a lot on Dave's side. Roger has not spoken to me since 1980. I was not privy to meetings they had. I just know that there was a very, very hard time indeed, with a lot of fighting.

GW Did you have a falling-out with Roger?

THORGERSON I don't know whether it was a falling-out. He didn't want to use me on *The Wall*, which is understandable. He was also supposedly cross with me for something, for a credit I'd given him in a book I'd done called *Walk Away, Renee*. An illustration of the *Animals* cover appeared in the book, and Roger didn't like the credit I'd given him. I corrected it on a reprint, so I don't know whether that was really what upset him.

GW You've done so much highly regarded work—not only for Pink Floyd but for other bands as well. Were you conscious at the time, or have you been conscious over the years, of raising the bar and setting certain standards for album design?

THORGERSON I don't think so. I understand your question, but I kinda don't think so, really. I think we were too busy working. You have to remember that for most graphic designers ... a large preoccupation may be your art, but another large preoccupation is called the next job. It's frightening, but it's useful. And it can drive you. You need to keep working and keep up your standards as much as you can; people might judge you only on your last job, in which case you might be out of work if you don't do as well as you can. You can do one job for somebody else and other people might call you, which is just what happened with Led Zeppelin. They saw a job I'd done for another band and rang up.

GW Which was that?

THORGERSON On an album called *Argus* by a British band, then popular, called Wishbone Ash. I think Jimmy [*Page*] saw it somewhere and rang up ... Actually, I think he got the manager—the infamous and late Peter Grant—to ring us up. That was pretty scary. [*laughs*] He rang up the studio, and me and my partner, Po [*Aubrey Powell*], had been acting like the Marx Brothers for the day. Peter Grant rang up and I did a sort of Groucho impersonation—badly, of course. And he was not amused. [*laughs*]

GW So what was working with Zep like?

The creative team who came up with the famous prism cover for *Dark Side of the Moon* (left-to-right): Roger Waters, Po (of Hipgnosis design) and David Gilmour.

THORGERSON It was considerably different. Po...did most of the direct communicating with them. We all did design and the work, but he did most of the communication. Zeppelin were not friends of ours from youth, so obviously the whole thing's different. But it was very great to work for Zeppelin. My son was very impressed we worked with Zeppelin; he actually reintroduced me to Zeppelin. It's easy to either over or, particularly, underestimate a band you're working with 'cause you're doing a job. You listen to them in order to gather impressions to make a picture, make a design, as opposed to listening to them as music to be enjoyed.

GW *In Through the Out Door*, the last of the five albums you did for Zeppelin, featured one of the most ambitious packages ever created. How did you come up with that?

THORGERSON In England, you often hear people say, "You don't need to expend all this effort on a cover. Why bother, man? The music sells itself. You can sell just as much in a brown paper bag." So for *In Through the Out Door*, we said, "Okay, we'll put it in a brown paper bag." And we did!

It was a lavish cover, actually. I enjoyed it a lot. Did you ever notice you could affect the dust jacket by putting water on it? If you applied spittle to it or a bit of water, it would change to color, like a children's coloring book we based it on. But we didn't tell anybody. I don't think Zeppelin told anybody, either.

GW What was the idea behind the object on the *Presence* cover?

THORGERSON It was inspired by the idea that somehow Zeppelin were really powerful. I think Zeppelin were a very particular band; they were very strong. The object was supposed to represent them. The idea was that everybody should feel that they needed this object, that it was so powerful that you couldn't live without it. You had to be exposed to this object wherever you were, perhaps once a day. And when you were exposed to it, it would zap you. Scientists would examine it, babies would hunger for it, ordinary families would sit around it. It was an all-purposeful, all-present, all powerful object.

GW How did you like working on Phish's new album, *Slip Stitch and Pass*?

THORGERSON I really enjoyed working for them. I hope we work again; boys, if you're listening, let's work again. I was very impressed by one particular piece of information: did you know that they don't work with a set list? You knew that? I didn't know that. How many rock bands do you know of that don't have a set list? I don't know any. I was really impressed by this, that they feel the level of communication with each other is such that they don't worry too much about what they're going to play. And they take things, take themes and improvise them, go off and play quite long versions of things. They seem to take an idea and run with it, musically speaking. I thought that was interesting.

GW Which would explain the cover.

THORGERSON It was about their improvisation. It's a picture of a man who's unraveling a very big ball of wool, and somehow it seemed to be appropriate—take an idea and run with it, see where it leads you.

GW How important is it for you to meet with a band in person? To see them perform live?

THORGERSON Essential. It is essential always to meet the band or musician in question, and always essential to hear the music and see them play, if I can. Sometimes I can't, because they won't be playing before a record is out. I've worked with very diverse musicians, Zeppelin on one hand and John McLaughlin on the other. I've worked for metal outfits and I've worked for Phish. And as diverse as the musicians are, so are the kinds of meetings we have had, not to mention where and when we met.

GW And how important is it for you to actually like the music that's on the albums you're designing?

THORGERSON That's a good question. I've had a couple of interesting arguments with other designers here on this particular point, and we agreed to differ. I took a decision quite early on, for right or for wrong, that I didn't make value judgments when I started to work. It seemed to me that this had the potential of putting one in a very tight corner. So I didn't judge. Give me a piece of music and I react to it—I don't have to like or dislike it. I find that music affects me; good or bad music, it has an effect on me. I just translate that effect from a sound spectrum into a visible eye spectrum.

I also find that my tastes change. If I were to turn down a job because I didn't like the music, I might like it later. Or vice versa. And there also will be those cases where even if you don't like their music so much, you'll think the musicians are great. Do you really want to turn to a great guy and say, "By the way, I can't work for you. Your music sucks." Maybe his music isn't so good this time around, but it might be great next time.

GW That's a very charitable and humane philosophy. Can you recall some instances where this actually happened to you?

THORGERSON [*laughs*] That I might give you for public consumption? Obviously, in a way, one would be very loath to say that. But notwithstanding the fact I might easily get litigated in your country or beaten over the head, I found working for Mike Oldfield very unsatisfying, not enjoyable. I don't think he enjoyed it, either. So there was something where I was interested in the music but not interested in the man. The other side of the coin would be a group called UFO. I would have to say that—chaps, I'm sorry if you're reading—I didn't really rate the music that highly, but the guys were great. They were really good fun.

I didn't like Led Zeppelin that much when I first worked for them, and I've worked on Floyd albums, like *Ummagumma*, that I don't like. I've worked on other albums, like *Meddle*, where I definitely didn't do near as good a job as the music.

GW How do you feel about doing album art in the CD age?

THORGERSON This is a continuing debate. The usual response of graphic designers is that the CD provides you with less of a graphic canvas to work on. But it has its own challenges. Also, designers are, to a great extent, realists; you've got to function, you've got to work. CDs are here. You've got to learn to like them. Obviously, though, I would rather have a bigger canvas. That's probably why I build big things sometimes. For Phish, I built this ball of yarn that is the size of a small house.

GW Part of the challenge seems to be in packaging, too, rather than simply designing a cover or a booklet.

THORGERSON I think designers are driven to do that because there's less of a canvas to work on with just the booklet. So where are they going to get their rocks off? Because it's smaller, it becomes more touchy, more of a tactile thing so that you can play more with textures and boxes and fold-outs and Digipaks—this pack, that pack, see-through trays, embossing, etc., etc. I have obviously indulged myself; I enjoyed greatly doing *Pulse* for the Floyd.

GW A spectacular CD package. How did that come about?

THORGERSON I think it came about for two particular reasons, one of which was that it was a live album. I wanted the package to be live, so we came up with a list of things that included balls and mazes. We had some that made a noise when you opened it, squeaked at you, some that smelled, others that you could see in the dark. And this one that had a flashing light thing, which reflected the heartbeat in *Dark Side*. And also it was a light, which is really handy 'cause obviously the Floyd have a really good light show. The other thing was that I was also fed up with having to squint at spine details. I thought, I'm going to make something that I know where it is when I want it. It was about a spine that was completely and utterly unique and recognizable, that says: "Here I am. You want to play me? I'm over here." I think it works really well. Mine still blinks.

GW I take it from your continued involvement with the Floyd that you view the current incarnation of the band as legitimate.

THORGERSON Yes, because Roger resigned. If you leave a band, I cannot see the moral imperative that would allow you to presume it finished. If you leave, you leave. And presumably a man of Roger's standing and intelligence left because that's what he wanted. I think it's peculiar because if it's not what he wanted, why did he do it? Nobody asked him to. Nobody pressured him to. So I presume he wanted to. But there was a lot of fighting afterward, so you have to presume that something went astray.

GW You chose the cover of *The Division Bell* to be the cover of your book. What's the special significance this piece has for you?

THORGERSON Obviously, we were tempted to choose *Dark Side* because of its success, but we eschewed that choice in favor of art. I hope it doesn't sound over-pretentious to say that. On a more simple level, this is the picture I have liked the most. It is the image I'm proudest of—at the moment. I think it says a lot about the Floyd. I think it says a lot about past Floyd. I think it says a lot about Roger. I think it says something about the layers of meaning, the elegance…the ghost, the spirit of Floyd. It says something about their ambiguities. It says all those things. It most particularly says something about departed friends.

GW And from your vantage point, do you think there is any truth to the rumors that Roger and the rest of the Floyd will be playing together again in the coming year?

THORGERSON [*laughs*] I've heard that. It sounds like bull to me. Although I think it would be quite interesting and dynamic if it did occur. I think you're talking about two huge talents here. And as much as there may have been friction, there's mileage to be made out of friction. But if you ask me if I think it's a reality—I don't think it's a reality. But then, of course, what's real and what's not with the Floyd?

Rik Sins/London Features

Roger Waters, solo artist

Revolver #3

In the Flesh

They've created some of the most profoundly depressing music in the history of rock, but Roger Waters and Nine Inch Nails frontman Trent Reznor are just tickled pink to shake hands.

By Alan di Perna

Roger Waters is waiting for Trent Reznor. "Presumably, they have to rouse him from a drug-induced coma," Waters dryly remarks. "These young rock stars…"

Just then Reznor turns up, and he's far from comatose. In fact, anticipation has driven him from his bed at an hour most unbecoming a rock star. "I woke up at 7:30 this morning," he confides. "I was going, 'God, I'm gonna talk to Roger Waters today!' "

The dean of arena rock drama meets the dark lord of industrial. As their colloquy gains momentum, one can feel Waters' frosty reservations slowly melting. He and Reznor really are kindred spirits.

They're both men who see the big picture, albeit a picture painted in somber tones. As the brooding masterminds behind Pink Floyd and Nine Inch Nails, respectively, Waters and Reznor hold a special place in the hearts of rock and roll misfits from ages, oh, 15 through 50. Pink Floyd's 1979 opus *The Wall* and NIN's 1994 album *The Downward Spiral* each depicts the slow, agonized unraveling of a psyche—the author's own, in each case, although thinly veiled by a plot line. *The Wall*'s Pink and *The Downward Spiral*'s nameless protagonist are characters who lapse into bleak solipsism—complete isolation from their fellow humans.

And that's how the public tends to think of both Reznor and Waters: withdrawn, melancholic, a wee bit misanthropic. Waters' acrimony toward his former bandmates in Pink Floyd is as legendary as Reznor's contempt for his former record label, TVT.

Our motive in bringing these artists together for the first time was to open up a dialogue between two of rock's major thinkers. Besides, who could pass up the opportunity of introducing the man who wrote *Animals* to the one who wrote, "I want to fuck you like an animal"?

REVOLVER Trent, maybe we could start by discussing the kind of role Roger's music has played in your own life and work.

TRENT REZNOR Well, I grew up on a farm in the middle of nowhere in Pennsylvania. And, not to sound too kiss-ass, but when *The Wall* came out it was a turning point for me. I was in high school at the time. And I remember that music had always been my friend— a companion, the brother I didn't have or whatever. I came from a broken home. I was alone a lot as a child. And when *The Wall* came out, that record seemed very personal to me, even though I was in a completely different lifestyle, place and situation than Roger would have been in at that time. I'd never heard music that had that sort of naked, honest emotion. I had that sense of, "Wow, I'm not the only person who feels this way." And when it came time to start writing my own music, after some failed attempts at generic lyrics, I realized that if I went inward and took journal entries and turned them into songs, that it seemed to strike a chord in others.

And then when I made my second album, *The Downward Spiral*, I aspired to start with a story. I tried to write songs that fit into the slots in the plot line. I soon realized how hard that is. I tried to abandon it. But when I got toward the end of the record, I realized I had kind of done that anyway—what I thought I couldn't do.

ROGER WATERS Forgive me, Trent. I don't know your work. I tend not to listen to rock and roll very much—if at all. But it sounds to me as if what you're doing fulfills all the functions that you've described in my work. There are still those kids on farms in the middle of Pennsylvania yearning to find some meaning in their own lives and discovering it—some of them at least—in music that could be described as underground, or at least not in the mainstream of popular culture.

REVOLVER You're both artists who have taken the full-length concept album as your main medium. Your work tends to make large statements about the human condition. What is it like to be doing that in the current musical climate, which seems to be one of disposability, one-off hit singles and short attention spans?

REZNOR It's very difficult, as I've discovered with my most recent record, *The Fragile*. It's a double album, and it's pretty dense. It takes about five or 10 listens to really get into it. As a fan, that's what I want when I buy a record—to dig in and go several layers deep. That's the thing about your work, Roger. If you look deeper, you find things.

WATERS But not everybody wants to go that deep.

REZNOR I fully understand that too. And I think there's something to be said for a nice appealing surface. But when you want to go looking for a deeper meaning, it ought to be there too. But nobody seems to have the time for that anymore. I guess from hiding in my studio for the past five years making *The Fragile*, I wasn't quite aware of how disposable the scene has become. It's a tough blow to withstand—just the way commercialism has turned music more into product than art. You're judged immediately by the first three weeks of your sales. And if it isn't what somebody at the record label said it would be, then it's a failure.

WATERS But don't you think it was always that way? All record companies are profit-orientated. The holy grail for them is to discover the mother lode of popular taste, in order that they should move huge numbers of product. And they were always that way, in my view. You know, there are these mythic kind of figures from the early days, like Sam Phillips. But Sam Phillips wouldn't have stuck with Elvis if people hadn't bought the records! "Popular" is an interesting word. I looked into it when I was doing a piece of writing recently. And in *The Shorter Oxford English Dictionary* one of the definitions of popular is "adapted to the popular taste."

REZNOR But are the record companies really catering to what the public taste is? Or do they, to a degree, dictate that taste to the public? MTV pumps their boy bands and their generic blond teenage icons to the masses. And I wonder how much of that is the public saying, "What are we supposed to like?" And they're bombarded with that.

WATERS I'm sure you're right. It's all very [novelist] Aldous Huxley. In fact, MTV is pure Big Brother. It's pure *Brave New World*. And there's no question but that those who make decisions about the way society works become the arbiters of the quality of human life. And in North America the general trend has been this: You find a piece of wilderness. If there are people or animals living on it, you kill them. Then you build a strip mall that contains a number of the most obviously successful and recognizable icons of the culture you're trying to spread over the land. So there's inevitably a McDonald's, a Sam Goody and all those things. I assume the reason for this is that it's convenient for the policy makers. It provides them with a system where there's plenty of cream floating around the top to be skimmed off. And I suppose the reason why the human race goes along with it is that, as yet, we don't know any better. That seems to be enough for most human beings. Although, if you ask most people, they don't actually feel a great sense of satisfaction in their lives, buying that dream.

It's interesting, Trent, that you should be voicing these concerns about this kind of stuff. I find myself not caring about that, really, or about the way the record industry is or what's going to happen to it. Maybe that's very selfish of me. But it may be that that wall of unconcern is almost necessary to some of the rest of us, in order that we should have a reference point to develop against.

REZNOR Right.

WATERS Something to rail against. You know, if we all lived in Sweden and our mums and dads all loved each other and everybody had sex all the time and the sun always shone—well, at least in summertime—and the sea sparkled and there was no pollution, then there might be no reason for anybody ever to do anything. It might be that we would never paint on the walls of the cave or write a novel or do anything, because we'd all be so content fitting into the great oneness of everything.

REZNOR I'm sure my output would be even less than it is now.

WATERS Is the human race goal-orientated? And if it is, what is the goal? Is it survival of the species? Is it more happiness for more of the people all of the time? Is it a kind of game where we measure the value of our lives in terms of how much we have or haven't succeeded materially? Or do we apply other measures, such as how much have we advanced spiritually during the time we had? These are questions we flirt with, from time to time, with the mathematics that is music, when it touches us. So it's interesting you talking about being on the farm and being touched by some piece of music or other. That's the bit that interests me. It's those moments when a person, whether it's Pythagoras or Trent Reznor, is touched by some organization of musical notes in some mathematical pattern, and discovers some connection either with another human being or with something about life that creates whatever it is in whatever part of the mind it is that you call emotion.

REZNOR That is the magic of music, to me. And what I discovered later—after being moved by music like yours, Roger, while growing up—is that my music was having the same effect on other people. Some would come up and say, "Man, you totally know what I'm going through. Your music helped me through this or that situation." But I only made that music to keep myself from going crazy, to get it out of my head. For me, there's a therapeutic value in conveying some possibly ugly or desperate or happy emotion. Sometimes it seems impersonal sitting in a dark studio with headphones on, trying to make a statement. But then a year later it's coming out of somebody's stereo across the world. And some emotional or spiritual circuit connects.

I've been grasping for what my purpose is here. Raised in isolation, on television, you're trained to behave a certain way. Expect certain things from life. I had a broken family. I didn't fit the mold. I wasn't the perfect individual I was told to be. I didn't fit in at school. I dropped out of college. And it wasn't really until I found my passion of music, and a way in which I could focus and channel my emotions, that I found my purpose in life. And then as an unexpected reward, in a way, I found out later that that I'm not the only person who feels that way. There are others out there. And maybe they felt better, like I did hearing your music years ago, Roger.

WATERS Yeah, maybe they did. I'm sure they did. There's room for all this stuff, though. I remember reading an interview with Ozzy Osbourne. I sat in an airport and I howled with laughter when I came to a wonderful section in this interview. I think he's living in California now. And they were asking him for money for his kids' school—to build a theater or whatever, the way they do. And he freaked out about it. He said, "I'm not giving you any fucking money. Why don't they ask all these fucking actors 'round here? They've all got more money than me anyway." And he said, "For fuck's sake, don't they understand? I'm the Prince of Darkness. I'm not fucking Neil Young!" And I just sat there and thought, How very cool. I dunno, there's something about that that appealed to me. Because it was so unprecious and unconcerned. And so out there and honest and in some way very cool. I like the idea of this guy. He sits in this strange middle-class state, having survived everything he has survived, railing against the forces of social concern.

REVOLVER Another thing that you two guys have in common is that you both are in the midst of preparing DVDs of your recent tours. What is it like encapsulating something like a rock and roll tour in this new medium?

REZNOR Roger, is your DVD basically your live show?

WATERS Yeah, it's the live show—and a documentary, if we can get it all on. Well actually, we can't get it all on. So I'm at the moment trying to persuade the record company to give the documentary away with the rest of the stuff. Because a DVD has limited space. So I'm under a lot of pressure to edit it—take stuff out.

REZNOR Make your product more appealing to the marketplace?

WATERS Yeah, exactly. We were under that pressure with the live album of the shows as well. "You should really put this out as a single CD, because it's more marketable." And I confess I did have a look at editing. I wrote a few song lists and I thought, I can't do this. This is ridiculous. So we persuaded the record company to sell a double CD at a reasonable price. I think live albums should be much less expensive than studio albums. The costs of making a live album are minimal, compared to a studio album. You just take a mobile to two or three gigs, record them, and choose the best bits.

REVOLVER Are you taking the same kind of approach on your DVD, Trent—a straight document of the show itself?

REZNOR That's the focus of this one. And I'm taking a very hands-on approach. In the past I've made the mistake of hiring "the guys who really know how to do this." What happens is your concert footage ends up looking just like everyone else's. So for this one, we just got seven good digital video cameras and filmed the last 10 shows of the tour from seven different perspectives: some locked-off shots, some handheld, a lot from the audience. To give a sense of what it was like to be there—in a nonprofessional kind of way. We adopted that same kind of attitude in post-production too. We thought we would edit it here in my studio on a Macintosh in Final Cut Pro. That led to, "Maybe we could adapt our studio for 5.1 surround sound," which we ended up doing. There have been a lot of hassles, but it's also been very educational.

WATERS You're lucky enough to be in a position where you can make those choices, which is great.

REZNOR Well, the timeline might be running out on that, given the sales of my last record. But I'm trying to keep as much in-house as possible. You see, I had a really bad experience with the first record label I was signed to. And when I finally got out of that situation and onto a new label I said, "Here's the deal. You give me a chunk of money and I'll give you a record. I don't want A&R. I don't want any interference. I'll give you magazine ads. I'll give you a video. I don't want your help." So that provided me with an in-house situation where I could do what I want without meddling fingers from record label strangers.

And now I'm trying to get this DVD done to meet what is a pretty unrealistic deadline. And trying to get my head around the fact that almost nobody is ever going to listen to this with the right setup. Most people can't set a stereo up, let alone six speakers with the right level balance and the right distance between speakers.

WATERS I actually think you're fighting a losing battle, trying to recreate anything like the experience of being at a rock and roll show with a DVD. Basically they're home movies. I regret not having made home movies of *The Pros and Cons of Hitch Hiking* and the *Radio K.A.O.S.* tours [*1984 and '87, respectively*]. And so I'm glad that I will have a home movie of the *In the Flesh* Tour 2000. I want to have it to put in a cupboard somewhere and maybe show to my grandchildren. But I don't know if it's something that interests me that much, I have to say. I don't really care about it.

REZNOR As far as re-creating the live experience?

WATERS Well, yeah. Frankly, I'd rather be fishing. Or reading. But you know, I'm 56 years old. How old are you?

REZNOR 35.

WATERS So it's kind of relative. There's 21 years difference. I might have cared more when I was 35. Not that I'm saying that you will eventually achieve fishing.

REZNOR I'm looking forward to it, actually.

WATERS After rock and roll comes fishing—I'm not saying that. But it takes a lot to get me in an environment where I have to be looking at video or film footage or a show and trying to make it look like a good home movie that I would be happy to sit and view in years to come. It's quite different than doing a show. I find putting together a live show consuming. Because it's the real thing. Not a recording of the real thing.

REZNOR Right, but don't you sometimes get that feeling that it's the last show of the tour and then it's gone? There's not a film somewhere that you can watch 10 years from now.

WATERS Absolutely. That's what I'm saying. I think some kind of document is important. But the important bit of the document is sometimes that few minutes of black-and-white film of Bob Dylan sitting backstage singing "How many roads must a man walk down," slightly off key, strumming a guitar and someone got it on a piece of 16 mil. Or John Lennon just sitting at a piano singing a song. At the end of the day, the bits that are interesting are the people and the songs. Not all the boogaloo. And maybe that's true of live shows too. It doesn't matter how much boogaloo there is. If it doesn't work with somebody sitting there, playing a guitar and singing the songs then it doesn't work, period. That's a personal view.

REZNOR I agree with you there.

WATERS But from the tenor of this conversation, it sounds like you're more involved in this stuff than I am.

REZNOR I suppose I can't help it. My first record came out 10 years ago. It unexpectedly touched a nerve. The second record got 10 times bigger than we ever thought it was going to be. We just happened to be in the right place at the right time. It propelled us

20 levels higher than we should have been, really.

WATERS You mean 20 levels more popular.

REZNOR Yeah. You find yourself being referenced by popular culture now.

WATERS Well, you do. But you can either choose to reference yourself like that, or not. And we all chose to do that, to a certain extent. If you're in rock and roll, you have to accept that part of the reason why you're there is because you like being patted on the back. Probably didn't get enough of it when you were kid. Certainly that's true of me. If we didn't have those needs we wouldn't be in rock and roll anyway.

REZNOR That's true. But I disappeared for five years to get my brain straightened out. I came back with a really dense double album that I think is the best I can do. But it's substantially different than what I've done in the past. It's not as obvious. And it sold well, but it didn't sell great. So now I'm settling into this … When I first started out, I'd ride around the country in a van 10 times if I needed to. I'd do interviews all day if I needed to…

WATERS But you sound confused by this, slightly.

REZNOR Well, I'm getting over the hump of realizing that I'm settling into what is right for me, artistically. But it might not be accessible for mass consumption.

WATERS Well, okay. So it's not. So you've recognized that. All you need to do is recognize that and then forget about it. Because it's uncontrollable. I think the one thing we all have to understand is that you can't go chasing the audience. That would be a living death for anyone who is serious about what they do. It sounds like you're agonizing about this stuff. And this is now me being wise after the event. I've been through the same agonies. But at the end of the day, I've had to understand that all you can do is your work. Maybe nobody will buy any of it. That could happen. You might make a record five years down the road and four people will buy it, you know?

REZNOR Right.

WATERS Modigliani never sold any pictures. Van Gogh was

peddling his pictures for a bowl of soup. Some of these geniuses never got any reward at all in their lifetimes. Except the reward that comes from doing your work and understanding your connection with the mathematics of life, or God, or whatever you want to call it.

REZNOR That's obvious to me. But it's really nice to hear you say that.

WATERS I've been through some of the same things, clearly. I've had a couple of big hit singles in my life, when I was with Pink Floyd. And I feel good about the work that I've done since then, particularly *Amused to Death* [1992]. I've sold a few records. Not big numbers. But that's just the way it is. The cool thing is the moment when you put that last brush stroke to the painting, stand back and go "Ahhhh." You know you've done good work. That's all you can expect. That's it. That's the end of it. If occasionally you get a letter from someone in Wisconsin saying "I like that song," or if tons of people go out and buy it and you get a big royalty check, well, that's great too. But it's not the big part of your equation. The big part is having found within yourself the ability to make the necessary connections to write the stuff and make a recording of it.

REVOLVER All these concerns about how your work is received by the public—do they become more acute, more stressful, when you're touring?

WATERS Not anymore for me. On my last tour the audiences were ages 15 through 50, but more 20-year-olds than anything else, as far as I could see. And they knew the songs. They like them. The songs have meaning to them. It was kind of a warm, touchy-feely experience for me. And I'm ashamed to say that I loved it. I'm now in a state emotionally where I can recognize, absorb and enjoy that connection with the audience. Where maybe 10 or 15 years ago, I couldn't. Because I was still essentially the tall guy in black, standing in the corner scowling at everyone—"Stay away. Leave me alone."

REZNOR I know that guy.

WATERS And I don't feel like that now. So it was fun. And we have really good relationships within the band, so I wasn't going through all that muck I went through with Pink Floyd.

REZNOR It's gotta feel good to look out and see an audience of some young people who are just discovering your music. Realizing that it has a timeless quality to it.

WATERS It's great. We're only just beginning to discover that about rock and roll. It didn't really start until the mid Fifties, so it's still a very young thing. And it may be that some of us will eventually turn into Duke Ellington or Louis Armstrong. The artists involved in rock and roll only have to get old enough for people to say, "Hey, what a big surprise. They lasted. It wasn't just an overnight teenage rebellion thing. It was jazz!" So there's room for what you and I do, Trent, and there's room for the boy bands and all the soft porn that's out there masquerading as rock and roll. Actually, it doesn't masquerade as rock and roll. It calls itself pop music. And I guess it was always that way.

REVOLVER Is it fair to say of both of you that your work takes a somewhat dim view of human nature?

REZNOR I'm focusing more internally in my work. I can't really say globally that I have a dim view of human nature. What has been the main impetus for me to sit and write has been a dissatisfaction with any number of topics based on my own personal perspective. And recently it hasn't been so much about "everything is terrible," as much as trying to make sense of my situation. I'm trying to find hope. I'm trying to find a way out, rather than digging myself deeper into a hole. So I don't feel my new album is overly pessimistic. It's less pessimistic than my last record. Relatively speaking, it's my positive record.

WATERS If you're optimistic enough to look for the good in yourself, then surely you must be optimistic enough to look for the good in others. And so I don't take a dim view of human nature. It seems to me there's a central question: Do human beings have a gestalt nature? If so, what is it? Are we capable of transcending the competitive elements in our nature so we can cooperate to the point where we might evolve into a species that lives even a tenth as long as the dinosaurs did? Who knows? It's an interesting question, seen within the context of 3,000 years of writing stuff down, and consequently 3,000 years of philosophy and research into language. Those 3,000 years are just a fraction of the time that human beings have been in existence. And now we're in the middle of a great mushrooming of the exchange of ideas and information. Of which rock and roll is just one small part. The whole Internet thing is fascinating for that reason alone. You know, it may be that the technology has arrived in our lifetimes to set us on the brink of whole new ways of looking at things. It may be that we will discover that the earth is not flat—in some other sense, of course. I mean it was only in the early part of the 15th century that Galileo was being persecuted. That's just a heartbeat ago, in terms of human history. So I think it's very easy to sit in the middle of being human here at the beginning of the 21st century and view things from a very narrow and parochial perspective. And not allow oneself to be open to larger issues.

REVOLVER Do either of you resent being portrayed in the media as gloomy purveyors of depressing music?

WATERS I really have nothing to say about that. That's not to say I don't care what people write about me. I do care a bit, although not much anymore. I know that I have been depressed sometimes. Maybe I will be again at times. But by and large I enjoy life and I empathize with other people. I hold that empathy to be the most valuable cornerstone of my life. And it may well be that that empathy translates into songs that sometimes aren't happy. But who cares, really? You don't choose what songs to write. My God, if we could all get up in the morning and say, "Hmm…what shall I write a song about today? Oh, I know. I'll write about young love. Or a flight to the moon. Or training puppies."

REZNOR Some people must be capable of that.

WATERS It's not like that—not for me anyway. You just get to a point where suddenly some feeling wells up in your breast and bursts its way out. A bit like *Alien*, you know? And there it is—a song. And I, for one, have precious little control over that. I look upon songwriting as a very passive exercise, really. I'm just really glad that it happens to me. 'Cause it feels great when it does.

REZNOR When Nine Inch Nails first got big, I got labeled as the most gloomy person in the world. And I realized that my own self-image was starting to become what I'd read about myself. Or how I was being treated by people around me, who only knew what they'd read about me. So it became a self-fulfilling prophecy. Because there was no time for rational thought in the madness of touring and not having a home. No time to get a perspective on how my life was changing—from poverty to wealth, from obscurity to being some sort of icon. In the end, it took some time to say, "Okay, who is really underneath all these layers of shit that have been built up?" From that point on, you realize that the media's just a game. The celebrity thing means nothing to me. It's more of an irritant than anything else.

WATERS About the time Pink Floyd really got popular—which was after *Dark Side of the Moon* [*1972*] and during *The Wall*, I guess—I just distanced myself from everything. On the *Animals* tour [*1977*] and the one before that we had a publicist and his job was to say no [*i.e., to interview requests*]. Just politely say no to everything. I did that for years and years. Looking back on those days, I'm so glad I refused to do *The Tonight Show*, refused to speak to Barbara Walters or do the covers of magazines. Particularly the chat show TV thing. I think if you start doing that stuff, you're saying to people, "Okay, I'm yours. Take me."

But the press have taken very little notice of me in my life. The music press have taken some notice. Some people have disapproved of what I've done and written negative things. All criticism is painful, always. I like good reviews and I don't like bad ones. But the "gloomy" label doesn't affect me much at all. Except for one thing. I'm writing a stage version of *The Wall*, and people ask me why I'm doing that. The reason is because I was never ultimately, completely satisfied with the record or with the movie. Because there are no laughs in either. And there were a lot of laughs in the story when I was living it. So recently I've been trying to write a version that has some laughs in it.

REVOLVER You also have an opera in progress, and a new rock album?

WATERS Yeah. I've got most of the songs for the new rock album now. I've just been working with the same band that I was working with on the road. I got them together in the studio, taught them the songs and we just worked on them. I think that's the way I'm going to proceed with this record. It's something I haven't done for years and years. Not since *Dark Side of the Moon*, really. We wrote the songs and actually toured *Dark Side of the Moon* before we recorded it. It's a good way for songs to evolve—to work with other musicians and see the way songs unfold in live performance.

And the opera is just a long, ongoing project. But I do now have soloists. It's just a question of finding time in their schedules. Boy, Trent, if you think our schedules are tight, you should be an opera singer. I think they all think their career is finite, even more than we do. The voice is an instrument that won't last forever. So while they can get the work they take it. Which makes their schedules very demanding.

REVOLVER I've heard a few different accounts of what the rock album is about. The war in Kosovo is one…

WATERS Well, that was just one song, which I did on the tour, called "Each Candle." And I thought that might be a central theme for the record. The idea of personal responsibility. In taking care of ourselves, we're taking care of each other at the same time. So if you make a beautiful mark on the great picture, then it's enough really. It's something.

REVOLVER But that might not be the entire theme?

WATERS No, all kinds of stuff is beginning to burst out, Alien-like, from my entrails. Which is good. But hey guys, *il faut partir*. I must go.

REVOLVER Thanks for doing this, Roger.

WATERS Hey, it's been a pleasure. And nice talking to you, Trent.

REZNOR Really nice, Roger.

WATERS Now I'm going to have to buy one of your records to see who you are.

REZNOR Maybe I'll even send you one.

WATERS That would be great. Why not all of them? That would be good. I look forward to hearing them.

WORLD

PRESENTS

Guitar World Presents is an ongoing series of books filled with extraordinary interviews, feature pieces and instructional material that have made *Guitar World* magazine the world's most popular musicians' magazine. For years, *Guitar World* has brought you the most timely, the most accurate and the most hard-hitting news and views about your favorite players. Now you can have it all in one convenient package: *Guitar World Presents*.

Guitar World Presents Alternative Rock
00330369 (352 pages, 6" x 9")...........................$17.95

Guitar World Presents Classic Rock
00330370 (288 pages, 6" x 9")...........................$17.95

Guitar World Presents Kiss
00330291 (144 pages, 6" x 9")...........................$14.95

Guitar World Presents Nü Metal
00330820 (160 pages, 6" x 9")...........................$14.95

Guitar World Presents Pink Floyd
00330799 (144 pages, 6" x 9")...........................$14.95

Guitar World Presents 100 Greatest Guitarists
00330960 (224 pages, 6" x 9")...........................$16.95

**Guitar World Presents Nirvana
and the Grunge Revolution**
00330368 (208 pages, 6" x 9")...........................$16.95

Guitar World Presents Metallica
00330292 (144 pages, 6" x 9")...........................$14.95

Guitar World Presents Van Halen
00330294 (208 pages, 6" x 9")...........................$14.95

Guitar World Presents Stevie Ray Vaughan
00330293 (144 pages, 6" x 9")...........................$14.95

FOR MORE INFORMATION, SEE YOUR LOCAL MUSIC DEALER,
OR WRITE TO:

HAL•LEONARD®
CORPORATION
7777 W. BLUEMOUND RD. P.O. BOX 13819 MILWAUKEE, WI 53213

Prices and availability subject to change without notice.
Some products may not be available outside the U.S.A.